# food family REPEAT

KEYSHAWN HUDSON

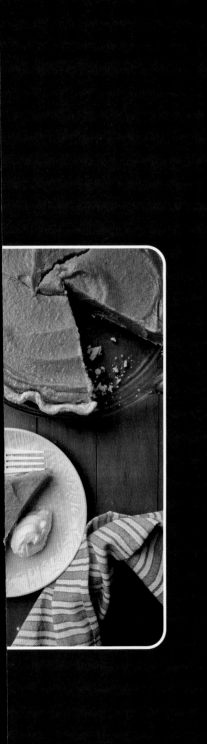

# food family REPEAT

**100** RECIPES FOR MAKING
EVERY DAY A CELEBRATION

**Publisher** Mike Sanders
**Art & Design Director** William Thomas
**Editorial Director** Ann Barton
**Senior Editor** Molly Ahuja
**Senior Designer** Jessica Lee
**Food Photographer** Daniel Showalter
**Food Stylist** Lovoni Walker
**Chef** Ashley Brooks
**Lifestyle Photographer** Tiffany Leu-Yen
**Food Stylist** Donna Noble
**Copy Editor** Claire Safran
**Proofreader** Lisa Starnes
**Indexer** Johnna VanHoose Dinse

First American Edition, 2024
Published in the United States by DK Publishing
1745 Broadway, 20th Floor, New York, NY 10019

The authorized representative in the EEA is Dorling Kindersley Verlag
GmbH. Arnulfstr. 124, 80636 Munich, Germany

A catalog record for this book
is available from the Library of Congress.
ISBN 978-0-7440-9485-5

DK books are available at special discounts when purchased
in bulk for sales promotions, premiums, fund-raising, or educational
use. For details, contact SpecialSales@dk.com

Printed and bound in China

**www.dk.com**

**Keyshawn Hudson (aka @chefkeysh)** is a full time content creator and recipe developer based in Lithia, Florida. He specializes in crafting recipes that are quick and affordable to make every day a celebration."

# dedicated to:

I dedicate this book to the people who helped shape me into the person I am today. Mom, I love you. You worked tirelessly to ensure I always believed in myself, despite anyone trying to bring me down. You put in twice the effort to lift me up. Dad, thank you for being my superhero. In my eyes, you are stronger than the Man of Steel himself. To Kevaughn, thank you for being your brother's keeper. I always feel safe with you because I know you always have my back. Lastly, thank you to Nina Dana. Though you are not here to witness this, this project is a tribute to the man you always believed I could become. Life is a beautiful story, and having the opportunity to share mine with all of you through this book is truly powerful.

# CONTENTS

## Introduction

## Anytime Apps

## Welcome to Jam Rock

## Soul Filled Holiday Season

## Southern Comfort

## Vegan Comfort

# INTRODUCTION

# INTRODUCTION

Food holds a profound significance for me that surpasses mere sustenance during times of hunger. At times, cooking has been my lifeline, fulfilling my quest for happiness and purpose that had spanned years. Throughout my life, I grappled with the question of, *why*?. I explored various avenues on my search for meaning, from sports to fashion, but nothing seemed to resonate. It wasn't until a realization struck me one day: My true passion had been right before my eyes all along. The love I have for food rescued me. Rising each day to cook for my loved ones and witnessing the joy on their faces offered me a newfound appreciation for life. I understand it may sound cliché, but cooking genuinely saved me.

The community of individuals who tune in daily to witness my culinary pursuits have been the greatest blessing I could have ever encountered. Thanks to their support, I have been given the opportunity to create projects like this very cookbook, enabling you to share the magic of my culinary creations with your loved ones as well. So, if you have ever found yourself in search of something more profound—a deeper meaning that permeates every aspect of your life, including your time spent in the kitchen—then through the pages of this cookbook, we'll embark on a culinary journey that transcends the mere act of cooking. Join me as we uncover the transformative power of food, nourishing not only our bodies but our souls, guiding us toward purpose, forging connections, and reigniting a passion for life.

This cookbook presents a harmonious fusion that caters to a diverse range of tastes and preferences. From effortless weeknight dinners to feed your family, to delightful appetizers perfect for sharing with friends, to vibrant vegan recipes and even slightly more intricate date night creations to savor with your significant other—there's something for everyone.

I've dedicated the past year to refining these recipes, sharing some through my online platform that has grown leaps and bounds over nearly three years. Cooking from the heart is my guiding principle, and I believe anyone who acquires this book shares that same sentiment.

The purpose of this cookbook is to empower readers to prepare meals crafted with love in their own kitchens and share them with the people they hold dear. While I'm entirely self-taught, one thing that no culinary institute can instill is a genuine passion for one's craft. As you immerse yourself in these pages and bring these recipes to life, that passion will naturally bloom within you. Cooking, for me, holds a profound connection to the home—a cherished tradition that I am grateful to share with you, so that you too can bring its warmth into your own home. This journey began with my extraordinary grandmother, whose greatest delight was feeding her beloved grandchildren. I can still vividly recall when I was a child, reaching out eagerly to collect hot steamed dumplings from her loving hands. That moment sparked an indescribable joy within me. However, it was when I moved to Jamaica at the age of nine to live with my dad that my culinary journey truly took flight.

My dad, the ultimate cook, has an unwavering passion for nurturing others. He not only grows his own produce but pours his heart into every dish he creates. Unbeknownst to him, he passed on that same love for nourishment to me. Inspired by the legacies of my grandmother and father, I am thrilled to feature a small collection of recipes from my Jamaican culture in this cookbook, inviting you to experience their flavors and traditions alongside me.

Cooking has been a part of my life for as long as I can remember. Even as a child in middle school, I took it upon myself to alleviate the burden from my parents' shoulders by preparing meals. It was my way of showing them how far I had come from being a mere observer. I was undeniably a foodie from the start—never straying far from the kitchen from the moment they started cooking until the final dish was ready. The flavors, techniques, and enticing scents fascinated me. Simply through observation, I gradually developed my own skills. It's no coincidence that my life and career have led me to this path. My passion was always there, an integral part of my journey.

To me, food and family are inseparable. Every accomplished executive head chef or revered tastemaker started in their own home, either nourishing their loved ones or being nurtured by them. Within the pages of this cookbook, I aim to honor that connection. Each recipe is crafted with love and carries a piece of my culinary journey, inviting you to experience the joy of cooking for your own family, just as I have. Together, let us celebrate the profound significance of food, family, and the remarkable journeys that emerge from the heart of our homes.

# ESSENTIAL TOOLS AND INGREDIENTS

On my culinary journey, I've discovered that the choice of ingredients and tools plays a pivotal role in crafting unforgettable dishes. Here, I'll share some of my preferences and offer insights into how and when to use them to elevate your cooking. Feel free to adapt these guidelines to your liking as you embark on your culinary journey with my cookbook.

## ESSENTIAL TOOLS

**Baking sheets and pans:** Useful for baking cookies, cakes, and other baked goods.

**Blender or food processor:** Useful for puréeing, blending, or chopping ingredients.

**Canisters or Food storage containers:** Essential for storing dry goods, leftovers, or meal-prepped ingredients.

**Can opener:** Essential for opening canned ingredients or canned goods.

**Cookware set:** It's very useful to have a set of pots and pans in various sizes for cooking different dishes.

**Chef's knife:** A versatile and sharp knife is useful for chopping, slicing, and dicing ingredients.

**Colander:** A perforated bowl is useful for draining cooked pasta or washing fruits and vegetables.

**Cutting board:** A sturdy surface is necessary for safely cutting and preparing food.

**Grater:** Used for grating cheese, vegetables, or spices.

**Kitchen timer:** Useful for keeping track of cooking and baking times accurately.

**Kitchen scale:** Ideal for precise measurement of ingredients by weight.

**Kitchen shears:** Handy for trimming herbs, opening food packages, or snipping string.

**Measuring cups and spoons:** Essential for accurately measuring dry and liquid ingredients.

**Mixing bowls:** It's useful to have various sizes of bowls for mixing ingredients and preparing sauces or dressings.

**Peeler:** Used for peeling the skin off fruits and vegetables.

**Oven mitts:** Essential for protecting your hands when handling hot dishes or pans.

**Strainer:** A fine-mesh sieve used for straining liquids or separating solids from liquids.

**Utensils:** Includes spatulas, tongs, wooden spoons, and slotted spoons for stirring, flipping, and serving food.

**Whisk:** Used for beating eggs, mixing sauces, or incorporating air into batters.

## ESSENTIAL INGREDIENTS

**Kosher salt:** I prefer kosher salt for its larger, flakier crystals, which make it easy to control seasoning. It's ideal for seasoning meats before cooking, but always remember to taste as you go for everything else.

**The Trinity (onions, celery, and bell peppers):** This trio forms the backbone of many of my recipes, especially in Cajun and Creole cuisine. Onions provide sweetness, celery adds a pleasant crunch, and bell peppers contribute a pop of color and flavor.

**Fresh herbs (basil, cilantro, parsley, thyme, and rosemary):** Fresh herbs can transform your dishes. Basil, cilantro, parsley, thyme, and rosemary are some of my favorites. Use them as a finishing touch to brighten up your dishes or incorporate them into marinades for added complexity.

**Garlic:** The aromatic and flavorful powerhouse, garlic, is a must-have in my kitchen. Crush, mince, or roast it to release its full potential. It's versatile and pairs well with almost anything.

**Dry granulated seasonings (paprika, cayenne, oregano, garlic powder, and onion powder):** Keep a variety of dry seasonings in your pantry for adding depth and complexity to your dishes. A lot of the time when you think you're missing flavor a little touch of a variety of granulated spices can really add to your dishes.

**Avocado oil:** A high-quality avocado oil is a versatile and heart-healthy alternative to olive oil. It's perfect for salads, dressings, and drizzling over finished dishes. It imparts a mild, buttery flavor that enhances the overall taste.

**Canola oil:** Canola oil is a neutral-flavored and high-heat cooking oil. It's great for frying, sautéing, and baking. Its light taste won't overpower your dishes, allowing the flavors of other ingredients to shine.

**Olive oil:** Olive oil is a staple in cooking, adding a rich and fruity flavor to salads, sautés, and marinades. It's a versatile and heart-healthy oil that complements a wide range of ingredients.

**Sesame oil:** Toasted sesame oil is a staple in Asian cuisine, adding a rich, nutty flavor to stir-fries, dressings, and marinades. Use it sparingly as a finishing touch for a delightful aroma and taste.

**Unsalted vs. salted butter:** Choose unsalted butter for better control over the salt content in your dishes. Salted butter is great for spreading on bread but can make your recipes overly salty.

**Heavy cream:** Heavy cream is a luxurious addition to sauces, soups, and desserts, adding richness and a velvety texture. It's a versatile ingredient that can turn ordinary dishes into extraordinary ones.

**Coconut milk:** This creamy and tropical ingredient is a must for curries, soups, and desserts. It lends a luscious, exotic flavor and a velvety texture to your dishes.

**Lemons and limes:** These citrus fruits are excellent for adding acidity and brightness to your recipes. Zest their peels for a burst of flavor and squeeze their juice into sauces and marinades.

**Dijon mustard:** Dijon mustard adds a tangy kick and depth of flavor to sauces, marinades, and vinaigrettes. It's a classic ingredient that enhances both savory and salad dishes.

**Honey:** Nature's sweetener, honey, is a fantastic way to balance flavors. Drizzle it over roasted vegetables, use it in marinades, or sweeten your beverages naturally.

**Cornstarch:** Cornstarch is a reliable thickening agent. Create a slurry by mixing it with cold water before adding it to sauces or soups for a smooth and glossy finish.

**Worcestershire sauce:** This savory and tangy sauce adds depth and umami to marinades, dressings, and various dishes. It's a secret weapon for enhancing the flavor of your recipes.

**Hoisin sauce:** Hoisin sauce is a sweet and savory condiment often used in Chinese cuisine. It's perfect for glazing meats, adding depth to stir-fries, and serving as a dipping sauce for spring rolls and dumplings.

# MEAL PREPPING:
## MY TIPS AND TRICKS

We all know that there never seems to be enough time in the day, especially for those of us trying to prioritize our work-life balance. That's why I've prepared a list of tricks that I use to adhere to a dietary schedule for myself and my family. Meal prepping can be time-consuming, but by following these tips, you can reduce the anxiety it causes by simplifying the process and breaking it down into manageable steps. Instead of viewing it as one daunting task, take it step-by-step.

**Invest in meal prep containers:** Get high-quality, airtight containers in different sizes to store your prepped meals. Choose containers that are microwave and freezer safe for easy reheating and storage. I personally like to use glass containers.

**Plan ahead:** Take some time to plan your meals for the week ahead. Consider your dietary goals, preferences, and any specific dietary requirements. Make a list of recipes and ingredients you'll need to shop for and what you already have on hand.

**Prep ingredients:** Wash, cut, and prep your ingredients in advance to save time during the week. Cut vegetables, portion out snacks, and precook grains and proteins to have them ready to go.

**Cook in bulk:** Choose recipes that can be easily scaled up to make larger portions. Cook a big batch of protein, such as chicken breasts or salmon, and a variety of grains and vegetables, like rice or roasted potatoes, that can be mixed and matched for different meals throughout the week.

**Portioning:** After cooking and/or prepping your food, divide your meals into individual portions to ensure you have balanced meals ready to grab.

**Store properly:** Store your prepped meals in the refrigerator or freezer based on their shelf lives. Be sure to date and use transparent containers to easily see what is inside and avoid any food waste.

**Don't be afraid to eat leftovers:** Make use of leftovers by incorporating them into new meals. For example, use leftover roasted chicken in salads, sandwiches, or wraps the next day.

**Enjoy the process:** Make meal prepping an enjoyable activity. Put on some music, involve your family members or friends, and experiment with new recipes and flavors to keep things exciting.

# ENTERTAINING:
## MY TIPS AND TRICKS

Feeding a crowd can be an anxiety-inducing task, but fear not! I have compiled a list to assist you in tackling it with ease, one step at a time. Preparation is key when it comes to cooking, and it goes beyond simply prepping the food. From setting the table to creating the perfect ambiance for your guests, every detail matters. However, it's important to remember that hosting does not have to be a stressful experience. Embrace and apply these tips to ensure a seamless experience for your next event. If you can do this, you'll be able to swiftly step out of the kitchen and savor the joy of being a gracious host, indulging in the amazing food you have prepared.

**Think ahead:** Start by creating a detailed plan for the occasion, including the number of guests, the menu selection, and a timeline of tasks. This will help you stay organized and avoid last-minute stress. Personally, I like to prepare anything the day before that I can. This can include pre-cutting vegetables, seasoning and marinating all proteins, and making any dish that can be served cold like potato salad or macaroni salad. This will elevate your efficiency and give you less to do the day of, thus alleviating stress.

**Simplify:** Craft a menu that includes dishes which can be prepared in advance or require minimal last-minute preparation. Consider a mix of make-ahead appetizers, slow cooker dishes, and easy-to-assemble desserts.

**Assign tasks:** Don't be afraid to ask for help! Assign specific duties to willing family members or friends. They can help you with setting the table, preparing a side dish, or managing the playlist. This will lighten your load and allow everyone to contribute to the event, which helps to foster stronger bonds and boost comradery.

**Prepping and execution:** Make a shopping list based on your planned menu to ensure you have all the ingredients and necessary supplies. I have a shopping list for every dish I have ever created, which allows me to get through my supermarket trips a lot smoother. You will want to do this sooner rather than later.

- Set up a buffet-style serving area to allow guests to serve themselves and reduce the need for constant attention to individual plates, allowing you to sit back, relax, and join in on the meal.

- Keep hot foods hot and cold foods cold by using chafing dishes, slow cookers, and ice-filled trays to maintain food safety and temperature.

- Have a designated area for trash and recycling to keep the space tidy and make cleanup easier. I use large Tupperware containers lined with a shopping bag to limit the number of times back and forth to the trash can.

**Set the mood:** Pay attention to the atmosphere by setting the mood with lighting, music, and decorations that suit the occasion. I personally love incorporating fresh flowers, candles, or themed decor to enhance the ambiance.

**Be a gracious host:** Greet your guests with a warm welcome, and ensure they feel comfortable throughout the event. Be attentive to their needs, offer refreshments, and engage in conversations to make everyone feel included and valued.

**Take breaks:** It's important to pace yourself and take short breaks when needed. Step away from the kitchen or entertaining space for a few moments to recharge and relax. It allows you to enjoy the gathering and interact with your guests without feeling overwhelmed.

# MENUS

## BAR FOOD FAVORITES

Cheesesteak Sliders with Keysh's Secret Sauce (see pages 46 and 201)

Wet Lemon Pepper Wings with Homemade Ranch Dressing (see pages 40 and 196)

Hot Honey Chicken Sandwiches with Steak Fries (see pages 125 and 117)

## GAME DAY ESSENTIALS

Crab Cake Bites with Homemade Remoulade Sauce (see pages 42 and 108)

Vegan Korean BBQ Wings served with Vegan Mac and Cheese
(see pages 125 and 117)

## FOOD COMA COMBINATIONS

Shrimp Fried Rice with Homemade Yum Yum Sauce (see pages 152 and 195)

Smoked Turkey & Collard Greens with Smothered Turkey Wings and
Corn Bread Dressing (see pages 92, 89, and 85)

Citrus & Herb Cream Cheese–Stuffed Salmon with Loaded Mashed Potatoes and
Bacon-Wrapped Asparagus (see pages 162, 190, and 172)

New York Strip with Mushroom Cream Sauce with Twice-Baked Jumbo Potatoes and
Honey Balsamic Brussels Sprouts (see pages 162, 190, and 172)

## DATE NIGHT DELICACIES

Parmesan-Crusted Chicken with Penne alla Vodka (see pages 160 and 159)

Honey Balsamic Lamb Chops with Loaded Mashed Potatoes and
Creamed Spinach (see pages 166, 186, and 180)

## CARIBBEAN SPICE SELECTIONS

Caribbean-Style Pepper Steak with Yellow Rice and Fried Ripe Plantains
(see pages 61, 185, and 73)

Oxtail with Jamaican Rice & Peas with Steamed Cabbage & Carrots
(see pages 62, 72, and 75)

**ANYTIME APPS**

# MOVIE THEATER QUESO DIP

**PREP TIME: 5 MINUTES • COOK TIME: 20 MINUTES**

I don't know about you, but when I go to the movies, I always stroll past the popcorn and go straight for the chips and hot queso dip. They're the ultimate comfort food for a movie night! This recipe takes the classic queso to the next level with a blend of pepper jack and cheddar cheeses along with spicy salsa verde, allowing you to enjoy a movie theater queso dip from the comfort of your own home. So grab some chips, put on your favorite film, and get ready for a cozy night!

## Serves: 4 people

2 tablespoons unsalted butter

2 tablespoons all-purpose flour

1½ cups whole milk

1 teaspoon garlic powder

1 teaspoon onion powder

½ teaspoon ground cumin

½ teaspoon chili powder

1 teaspoon smoked paprika

1½ teaspoons kosher salt

½ teaspoon freshly ground black pepper

4 ounces (113g) shredded cheddar cheese

4 ounces (113g) shredded pepper jack cheese

1 tablespoon store-bought or homemade salsa verde

1. To a medium skillet or saucepan over medium-low heat, add the butter. Once melted, whisk in the flour and cook until light brown.

2. Gradually add the milk while whisking to break down any clumps.

3. Stir in the garlic powder, onion powder, ground cumin, chili powder, smoked paprika, salt, and pepper. Once the mixture begins to thicken, reduce the heat to low or turn it completely off. Add the cheddar and pepper jack, stirring until smooth and consistent.

4. Stir in the salsa verde until well combined.

5. Transfer the dip to a serving bowl. Serve with my Homemade Tortilla Chips (page 30) and enjoy.

# ONE-SKILLET CHORIZO & CHEESE DIP

**PREP TIME: 10 MINUTES • COOK TIME: 25 MINUTES**

Cheese dip is one of the easiest appetizers out there to make—and why not make it even better by combining it with spicy and savory chorizo? This flavor-packed bowl of creamy, cheesy goodness is perfect for any event! Just serve it up with some tortilla chips (page 30) and you'll have the crowd going wild at the next get-together.

## Serves: 8

1lb (454g) hot chorizo, removed from the casings

1 can (10oz [285g]) of diced tomatoes with green chilies

½ cup shredded cheddar cheese

½ cup shredded Monterey jack cheese

8oz (227g) Velveeta, cubed

8oz (227g) cream cheese, softened

½ cup sour cream

2 tablespoons minced fresh cilantro

1. Preheat the oven to 350°F (180°C).

2. To a large cast-iron skillet over medium heat, add the chorizo and cook for 8 minutes, breaking it up into smaller pieces as it cooks through.

3. Remove the skillet from the heat and add the diced tomatoes with green chilies, cheddar, Monterey Jack, Velveeta, cream cheese, sour cream, and cilantro.

4. Place the skillet in the oven and bake for 15–20 minutes or until the cheese is melted and bubbly.

5. Remove the skillet from the oven and serve the dip hot with Homemade Tortilla Chips (page 30).

# BUFFALO CHICKEN DIP

**PREP TIME: 15 MINUTES • COOK TIME: 40 MINUTES**

There aren't many dishes you can't add buffalo sauce to and not increase the flavor a few notches, but the most famous of all has to be a buffalo chicken dip. Made with seasoned shredded chicken and cream cheese melted together with gooey mozzarella and rich Parmesan cheese, this dip creates something dangerously addictive. If you want to get even crazier, add some blue cheese to the top for a tangy twist. This recipe is so delicious and so easy to make, you have to try it out!

## Serves: 4–6

1lb (475g) boneless, skinless chicken breasts

1 teaspoon smoked paprika

2 teaspoons garlic powder

2 teaspoons onion powder

2 teaspoons chili powder

2 teaspoons seasoned salt

2 tablespoons avocado oil

1 cup diced white onion

3 garlic cloves, minced

½ cup thinly sliced green onion

1 tablespoon ranch seasoning

8oz (227g) cream cheese

½ cup sour cream

½ cup ranch dressing

1 cup buffalo sauce

¾ cup shredded mozzarella, divided

¾ cup grated Parmesan, divided

1. Preheat the oven to 350°F (180°C).

2. In a large bowl, combine the chicken breasts, smoked paprika, garlic powder, onion powder, chili powder, and seasoned salt. Mix well to coat.

3. To a large cast-iron skillet over medium heat, add the avocado oil. Once hot, sear the chicken for 4 minutes on each side.

4. Use two forks to pull and shred the meat. (It should look like pulled pork when finished.)

5. Once the chicken has been pulled apart, add the white onion, minced garlic, and green onion. Sauté until soft, then add the ranch seasoning.

6. Transfer the cooked chicken and everything else in the skillet to a large bowl. Add the cream cheese, sour cream, ranch dressing, buffalo sauce, ½ cup of mozzarella, and ½ cup of Parmesan. Mix until well combined and add to a cast-iron skillet or baking dish. Top the dip with the remaining ¼ cup of mozzarella and the remaining ¼ cup of Parmesan.

7. Place the skillet in the oven and bake for 25 minutes.

8. Remove the skillet from the oven and allow it to cool for 20 minutes before serving with your favorite chips or sliced bread.

# SPICY CRAB DIP

**PREP TIME: 15 MINUTES • COOK TIME: 45 MINUTES**

Who says seafood and cheese can't go together? Because this spicy crab dip will change their mind. Anyone who loves spice will be a fan of the subtle flavor of crab meat mixed with Cajun spices and cheesy goodness. Not only is it a quick fix, but this dip is also that "something different" you have been looking for to serve your guests at the next party.

## Serves: 4–6

7 tablespoons unsalted butter, divided

¼ cup diced jalapeño

¼ cup diced sweet onion

¼ cup diced red bell pepper

1 tablespoon Tony Chachere's Original Creole seasoning

8oz (227g) cream cheese

½ cup sour cream

Juice of ½ lemon

1 tablespoon Worcestershire sauce

2 teaspoons Louisiana Hot Sauce

2 teaspoons Old Bay seasoning

8oz (227g) lump crabmeat

¼ cup grated Parmesan

¼ cup Colby-Jack cheese, plus more

1 French baguette

3 garlic cloves, minced

¼ cup chopped fresh parsley

1. Preheat the oven to 350° (180°C).

2. To a small skillet over medium heat, add 3 tablespoons of unsalted butter. Once melted, add the jalapeño, onion, and bell pepper. Sauté until soft.

3. Stir in the creole seasoning, cream cheese, and sour cream. Mix until well combined.

4. Add the lemon juice, Worcestershire sauce, hot sauce, and Old Bay seasoning. Mix until well combined.

5. Add the crabmeat, Parmesan, and Colby-Jack. Mix until well combined.

6. Place the mixture in a large cast-iron skillet or regular baking dish. Coat the top with as much Colby-Jack as you prefer.

7. Place the skillet in the oven and bake for 25 minutes or until slightly charred and bubbly. Remove the skillet from the oven and let it sit for 15 minutes.

8. In a microwave-safe bowl, combine the garlic, parsley, and remaining 4 tablespoons of butter. Microwave on high for 60 seconds or until the butter is fully melted. Evenly brush the melted mixture on the top of the baguette.

9. Place the baguette on a baking sheet, place the sheet in the oven, and toast the bread for 10 minutes.

10. Remove the sheet from the oven, slice the baguette, and serve with the dip.

# HOMEMADE TORTILLA CHIPS

**PREP TIME: 10 MINUTES • COOK TIME: 20 MINUTES**

What if I told you that you could make fresh tortilla chips at home in under 30 minutes? With this recipe, you absolutely can! And as we all know, no dip is complete without a side of chips. These homemade tortilla chips pair perfectly with all the delicious dips included in this cookbook, so you can impress your guests with a snack that's not only easy to prepare but also incredibly tasty. Your guests will be amazed when they ask where you bought these chips and you can proudly say, "They're homemade!"

## Makes: 60 tortilla chips

Vegetable oil, for frying

15 corn tortillas

Kosher salt, to taste

2 teaspoons chili powder (optional)

1. To a large frying pan or deep pot, add about 2–3 inches (5 to 7.5cm) of vegetable oil. Heat it until it reaches 350°F (180°C).

2. Cut each tortilla into 4 equally sized triangular quarters. Working in small batches, fry the tortillas until they're a toasty golden color.

3. Transfer the fried tortillas to an elevated wire rack to drain the excess oil. While still hot, salt the tortilla chips and sprinkle chili powder (if using) over the top.

4. Serve with all the amazing dip recipes included in this cookbook and enjoy!

# GUACAMOLE

**PREP TIME: 15 MINUTES • COOK TIME: NONE**

Fresh guacamole is super easy to make! With just 15 minutes of vegetable preparation, you can whip up a bowl of tasty guacamole for your friends and family in no time. The freshness of the tomatoes and onions combined with spicy jalapeños and ripe avocados—all tied together with lime juice—make for an unforgettable party appetizer. This is something no one will stop eating until it's all gone.

## Makes: 3-4 cups

4 ripe avocados

1½ medium tomatoes, diced

2 jalapeños, seeded and diced

½ cup diced red onion

¼ cup diced white onion

¼ cup chopped fresh cilantro

Juice of 2 limes

Kosher salt and freshly ground black pepper, to taste

1. Cut the avocados in half, remove the pits, and use a spoon to scoop out the avocado flesh. In a large bowl, combine the avocados and the remaining ingredients. Use a potato masher or fork to partially mash the ingredients, leaving small chunks for texture.

2. Taste and adjust the seasoning to your preference.

3. Serve with Homemade Tortilla Chips (page 30) and enjoy!

# SPINACH & ARTICHOKE DIP WONTONS

**PREP TIME: 30 MINUTES • COOK TIME: 15 MINUTES**

What's a party without spinach artichoke dip? Spinach artichoke dip is always the first to go at my gatherings, so I had to come up with a way to make it even better. Then it hit me! Put it in wonton wrappers, deep-fry them, and serve! They're such a unique appetizer and make for a fun twist on the same old boring dip we've been eating for years.

### Makes: 20-30 wontons
### Serves: 10

1 tablespoon avocado oil

½ white or yellow onion, diced

4 garlic cloves, minced

3 cups baby spinach, roughly chopped

8oz (227g) cream cheese, softened

½ cup sour cream

½ cup grated Parmesan

½ cup mozzarella

½ cup drained and chopped artichoke hearts

½ teaspoon kosher salt

1 teaspoon onion powder

1 teaspoon garlic powder

½ teaspoon freshly ground black pepper

1 package of wonton wrappers

Vegetable oil, for frying

1. To a large skillet over medium heat, add the avocado oil. Once hot, add the onion and garlic, and sauté until fragrant.

2. Add the spinach and cook until soft and shrunken.

3. In a large bowl, combine the sautéed onion, garlic, spinach, and the remaining ingredients except for the vegetable oil. Mix until well combined.

4. Place a wonton wrapper flat on an even surface and add a spoonful of the spinach and artichoke mix in the middle. Use your fingers to wet the edges of the wrapper with water. Fold the wrapper in half, creating a triangle, and press the edges together to seal. Repeat this step until you've used all the mix.

5. Add 3 inches (7.5cm) of vegetable oil to a large pot and heat it to 350°F (180°C). Working in small batches, fry the wontons until golden brown.

6. Transfer the wontons to a plate lined with paper towels and then place them on a platter for serving.

# JERK CHICKEN TAQUITOS WITH AVOCADO CREMA

**PREP TIME: 25 MINUTES (PLUS REFRIGERATION TIME) • COOK TIME: 25 MINUTES**

Jerk chicken taquitos give you everything you love about the Caribbean flavor of jerk chicken wrapped in a crunchy Mexican taquito. To top it all off, I paired them with a fresh avocado crema that gives you a tangy contrast to mellow out the kick of the jerk seasoning. The combination is a match made in heaven!

## Makes: 10 taquitos and 1 cup of avocado crema

### FOR THE TAQUITOS

1lb (454g) boneless, skinless chicken thighs

1 tablespoon jerk seasoning

1 teaspoon kosher salt

1 teaspoon garlic powder

2 tablespoons avocado oil

8 ounces (227g) shredded Monterey jack cheese

2 tablespoons chopped fresh cilantro

1 tablespoon freshly squeezed lime juice

10 small flour tortillas

Vegetable oil, for frying

### FOR THE CREMA

½ cup sour cream

Juice of 1 lime

2 tablespoons chopped fresh cilantro

2 ripe avocados, peeled and pitts removed

1 teaspoon garlic powder

1 teaspoon kosher salt, plus more to taste

1 teaspoon chicken bouillon powder

Freshly ground black pepper, to taste

1. In a large bowl, combine the chicken thighs, jerk seasoning, salt, and garlic powder. Mix until well combined. Cover and refrigerate for 2–24 hours.

2. To a large cast-iron skillet over medium heat, add the avocado oil. Once hot, sear the chicken on both sides until fully cooled, about 6 minutes per side.

3. Place the chicken on a cutting board and use a fork to shred the meat. Add the chicken to a large bowl.

4. Place a flour tortilla flat on a clean counter or cutting board. Add a small amount of shredded chicken, Monterey Jack, cilantro, and a squirt of lime juice. Ensure to evenly spread the ingredients across the tortilla. Roll the tortilla tightly. Repeat this step until you've used all 10 tortillas.

5. In a large cast-iron skillet over medium heat, add 1 inch (2.5cm) of vegetable oil for a shallow fry. Heat the oil to 350°F (180°C).

6. Working in batches, fry the taquitos until golden brown and crunchy. Transfer the taquitos to an elevated wire rack to drain the excess oil, giving them a crispier finish.

7. To make the avocado crema, combine all the ingredients in a blender. Blend on high speed until smooth. Transfer the crema to a serving bowl.

8. Dip a crispy jerk chicken taquito in the flavorful avocado crema for the perfect bite every time!

# CHICKEN, BACON & RANCH FRENCH BREAD

**PREP TIME: 15 MINUTES • COOK TIME: 20 MINUTES**

Chicken, bacon, and ranch are ingredients that were just made for each other—and adding them to French bread takes the experience up another notch. This is the perfect recipe for anyone looking to feed a large group in a short amount of time. Serve with ranch or marinara sauce for a standout appetizer for your friends and family.

## Serves: 4–6

1 large French bread loaf

4 tablespoons unsalted butter, softened

4 garlic cloves, minced

¾ cup shredded cooked rotisserie chicken breast

¾ cup crumbled cooked bacon (or use bacon bits)

1 cup shredded part-skim mozzarella

¼ cup grated Parmesan

½ cup ranch dressing, plus more

2 tablespoons chopped fresh parsley (optional)

1. Preheat the oven to 375°F (189°C). Line a baking sheet with aluminum foil.

2. Cut the French bread loaf in half lengthwise and place the halves face up on the prepared baking sheet.

3. In a small bowl, combine the butter and garlic. Evenly spread this mixture over the French bread.

4. Add the shredded chicken and bacon. Top with the mozzarella and Parmesan.

5. Place the sheet in the oven and bake until the cheese is fully melted and toasty, about 15–20 minutes.

6. Remove the sheet from the oven. Drizzle the halves with ranch dressing and sprinkle chopped parsley (if using) over the top.

7. Once cool, slice the French bread and serve with more ranch dressing.

# BUFFALO CHICKEN TENDERS

**PREP TIME: 20 MINUTES (PLUS MARINATING TIME) • COOK TIME: 20 MINUTES**

This simple yet staple appetizer for a big game day or a party with family and friends has a crunchy fried chicken goodness paired with a spicy buffalo sauce you won't be able to get enough of. Serve them up with some homemade French fries or even by themselves for a guaranteed hit at your next gathering.

## Serves: 4–6

3 large eggs

2 lbs (907g) chicken tenders

Canola oil, for frying

1 cup all-purpose flour

½ cup panko breadcrumbs

2 teaspoons garlic powder

2 teaspoons onion powder

2 teaspoons smoked paprika

1 teaspoon chili powder

2 teaspoons kosher salt

1 teaspoon freshly ground black pepper

2 teaspoons chicken bouillon powder

1 cup buffalo sauce

1. In a large bowl, beat the eggs. Add the chicken tenders to the eggs. Cover and refrigerate to marinate for 2 hours.

2. To a Dutch oven or large pot, add 3 inches (7.5cm) of canola oil and heat it to 350°F (180°C).

3. In a separate large bowl or dish, combine the flour, breadcrumbs, garlic powder, onion powder, smoked paprika, chili powder, salt, black pepper, and bouillon powder. Evenly coat each tender in the flour mixture, shaking off any excess.

4. Working in small batches, deep-fry the chicken for 6–8 minutes or until golden brown and crispy.

5. Transfer the fried chicken tenders to an elevated wire rack to drain the excess oil.

6. To a small bowl, add the buffalo sauce and chicken tenders. Toss until fully coated.

7. Serve with my Homemade Ranch (page 196) or your favorite blue cheese dressing.

# WET LEMON PEPPER WINGS

**PREP TIME: 10 MINUTES • COOK TIME: 35 MINUTES**

Wet Lemon Pepper Wings is a clever name for a wing sauce that combines the flavors of buffalo wings with the zesty taste of lemon pepper. No game day is complete without a big bowl of hot wings, and this recipe is exactly what your friends and family need to please their taste buds at every gathering. The deep-fried crunch of the wings, paired with the spicy kick of the homemade sauce, is a guaranteed hit.

## Makes: 12 wings, depending on size

2 lbs (907g) chicken wings, drums and flats separated using a cleaver or sharp chef's knife

1 teaspoon garlic powder

1 teaspoon onion powder

1 teaspoon chili powder

1 teaspoon ground cayenne

½ cup baking powder

Vegetable oil, for frying

2 tablespoons unsalted butter

¼ cup honey

¼ cup buffalo sauce

1 tablespoon freshly squeezed lemon juice

1½ tablespoons lemon pepper seasoning

1. Pat the chicken wings dry with paper towels. In a large bowl, combine the wings, garlic powder, onion powder, chili powder, and cayenne. Mix well to coat. Add the baking powder and mix again.

2. To a large pot or Dutch oven over medium-high heat, add 4 inches (10cm) of vegetable oil and heat it to 350°F (180°C).

3. Working in small batches, fry the wings for 12 minutes or until golden brown. Transfer the wings to an elevated wire rack to drain the excess oil.

4. In a medium nonstick skillet or saucepan over low heat, melt the unsalted butter. Whisk in the honey, buffalo sauce, lemon juice, and lemon pepper seasoning. Whisk until the sauce becomes silky.

5. Add the wings to a large bowl and coat them generously in the sauce.

6. Serve with ranch or blue cheese dressing and enjoy!

# CRAB CAKE BITES

**PREP TIME: 20 MINUTES (PLUS REFRIGERATION TIME) • COOK TIME: 10–12 MINUTES**

I'm an island boy at heart, so I love all types of seafood, especially crab cakes. And if you love crab cakes, you'll love these deep-fried crab cake bites. This recipe combines everything you love about a Maryland-style crab cake, then takes it to the next level by deep-frying it in a seasoned breading and serving it up with my remoulade sauce (page 198).

## Makes: 25–30 crab cake bites, depending on size

### FOR THE CRAB MIX
¾ cup mayonnaise

1 tablespoon Dijon mustard

½ tablespoon Worcestershire sauce

1 tablespoon Louisiana Hot Sauce

Zest of ½ lemon

Juice of 1 lemon

3 large eggs, beaten

½ red bell pepper, diced

1 large shallot, diced

1 lb (454g) jumbo lump crabmeat

1 cup seasoned breadcrumbs

2 teaspoons Old Bay seasoning

1 teaspoon smoked paprika

Kosher salt and freshly ground black pepper, to taste

Vegetable oil, for frying

1 batch Remoulade Sauce (see page 198), for serving

### FOR THE COATING
1 cup all-purpose flour

1 teaspoon garlic powder

1 teaspoon onion powder

2 large eggs, beaten

2 cups breadcrumbs

1. In a large bowl, whisk together the mayonnaise, Dijon mustard, Worcestershire sauce, hot sauce, lemon zest and juice, and 2 eggs. Whisk until smooth and consistent.

2. Add the bell pepper, shallot, crabmeat, Old Bay seasoning, smoked paprika, and salt and pepper to taste. Mix until evenly combined.

3. Use an ice cream scoop or your hands to form the crab cake mixture into small balls. Place each ball on a tray lined with parchment paper and refrigerate for 1 hour.

4. In a small bowl, combine the flour, garlic powder, and onion powder. Mix well.

5. To a second small bowl, add the remaining 2 eggs. To a third small bowl, add the breadcrumbs. Coat the crab bites in the flour mixture, then in the eggs, and lastly in the breadcrumbs.

6. To a Dutch oven or large pot over medium–high heat, add 2–3 inches (5 to 7.5cm) of vegetable oil. Once the oil reaches 350°F (180°C), fry the crab bites for 3 minutes or until golden brown.

7. Transfer the crab bites from the oil to an elevated wire rack to drain the excess oil. Serve with the Remoulade Sauce.

# CHEESE & BEEF EMPANADAS

**PREP TIME: 25 MINUTES • COOK TIME: 20 MINUTES**

These empanadas are an easy but delicious appetizer that will keep your guests coming back for more. The flavorful and juicy ground beef, seasoned with Hispanic household classics like sofrito and Sazón, is encased in a crunchy empanada dough that will give you a bite you'll never forget. Make sure you make enough—they won't last long!

## Makes: 10–15 empanadas, depending on size

1 tablespoon avocado oil

1lb (454g) lean ground beef

1 white onion, diced

½ green bell pepper, diced

5 garlic cloves, minced

2 teaspoons Sazón seasoning

2 teaspoons adobo seasoning

1 tablespoon store-bought or homemade sofrito

2 tablespoons tomato paste

1 package of store-bought empanada dough

1 cup shredded cheddar cheese

Vegetable oil, for frying

1. To a large nonstick skillet over medium heat, add the avocado oil. Once hot, brown the ground beef, breaking up large chunks as it cooks.

2. Add the onion, bell pepper, and garlic. Cook until fragrant and soft.

3. Stir in the Sazón and adobo seasonings, sofrito, and tomato paste. If needed, thin the mixture with a touch of water.

4. Place one piece of empanada dough on a cutting board or clean surface. Place a spoonful of the ground beef mixture and a sprinkle of cheese in the center of the dough. Fold the dough over, enclosing the beef in the center, then use a fork to crimp the edges.

5. Repeat until you've used all the filling.

6. To a large pot or Dutch oven over medium heat, add 3 inches (7.5cm) of vegetable oil and heat it to 350°F (180°C).

7. Working in small batches, fry the empanadas for 3 minutes or until golden brown.

8. Transfer the empanadas to an elevated wire rack to drain the excess oil.

9. Serve hot and enjoy.

# CHEESESTEAK SLIDERS

**PREP TIME: 15 MINUTES • COOK TIME: 20 MINUTES**

These sliders are a staple for any game night or gathering. They're a fun and quick way to enjoy the iconic flavors of a classic Philly cheesesteak in finger-food form. From the juiciness of the thin ribeye steak cooked down to perfection with onions, peppers, and mushrooms to being finally closed together in a garlic butter–topped slider bun with provolone and white American cheese, you'll find no better bite out there.

## Makes: 12 sliders

2 tablespoons avocado oil

1 green bell pepper, sliced

1 onion, sliced

1 cup white mushrooms, sliced

1lb (454g) thinly sliced ribeye

2 teaspoons garlic powder

1 teaspoon onion powder

Kosher salt and freshly ground black pepper, to taste

Chipotle-Lime Mayonnaise (see page 205) (optional)

6 slices white American cheese

6 slices provolone

2 tablespoons unsalted butter

2 garlic cloves, minced

1 tablespoon minced fresh parsley

12 slider buns

1. Preheat the oven to 350°F (180°C). Line a baking sheet with aluminum foil.

2. To a large cast-iron skillet over medium heat, add the avocado oil. Once hot, add the bell pepper, onion, and mushrooms. Sauté until tender. Remove them from the skillet and set aside.

3. To the same cast-iron skillet, add the sliced ribeye. Season with the garlic powder, onion powder, and salt and pepper to taste. Cook the ribeye until browned, about 3–4 minutes.

4. Cut the slider buns in half and place them on the prepared baking sheet. To assemble the sliders, add the ingredients to the bottom bun in this order:
   - Chipotle-lime mayomaise (optional)
   - White American cheese
   - Cooked ribeye
   - Sautéed veggies
   - Provolone

5. Add the top buns on top then place the sheet in the oven and cook until the cheese melts.

6. In a microwave-safe bowl, combine the butter, garlic, and parsley. Microwave on high for 60 seconds, or until the butter is melted.

7. Generously brush the top buns with the garlic butter. Continue cooking until the top buns become slightly toasted.

8. Transfer the cheesesteak sliders to a serving platter. Serve with ketchup, mayo, or mustard for dipping.

# BABY SHOWER MEATBALLS

**PREP TIME: 20 MINUTES • COOK TIME: 25 MINUTES**

Looking for a sweet and savory appetizer to serve at your next family function? Look no further—I saved the best one for last! Baby Shower Meatballs are a classic. The ingredients are simple, but when mixed together, you won't be able to stop eating. The grape jelly combined with the subtle flavors of a juicy meatball gives this bite-sized appetizer the perfect amount of tanginess that will keep everyone asking for more.

## Makes: 20 meatballs, depending on size

### FOR THE MEATBALLS

1 lb (454g) ground beef

½ cup seasoned breadcrumbs

¼ white or yellow onion, diced

2 chili peppers, seeded and diced

¼ cup minced fresh parsley

2 tablespoons soy sauce

1 large egg

2 teaspoons kosher salt

½ teaspoon freshly ground black pepper

1 teaspoon garlic powder

1 teaspoon onion powder

1 teaspoon smoked paprika

2 tablespoons avocado oil

### FOR THE SAUCE

1 cup store-bought barbecue sauce

¼ cup ketchup

½ cup grape jelly

1 tablespoon apple cider vinegar

¼ cup soy sauce

¼ cup honey

3 tablespoons hoisin sauce

2 tablespoons Worcestershire sauce

Kosher salt and freshly ground black pepper, to taste

1. Preheat the oven to 400°F (200°C). Line a baking sheet with parchment paper.

2. To make the meatballs, in a large bowl, combine all the ingredients. Mix until well combined.

3. Use your hands or an ice cream scooper to form the ground beef mixture into 2-inch (5cm) balls. Place them on the prepared baking sheet.

4. To a large skillet or cast-iron pan over medium heat, add the avocado oil. Once hot, add the meatballs to the pan and sear, in batches, until they are 75% of the way done, about 6–8 minutes. Move the meatballs back to the baking sheet.

5. To make the sauce, add all the ingredients to the skillet or pan that you used to sear the meatballs. Whisk over medium heat until fully combined and heated through.

6. Turn off the heat and add the meatballs back to the pan. Toss to coat them in the sauce. Move the meatballs back over to the baking sheet.

7. Place the baking sheet in the oven and bake the meatballs for 25 minutes or until fully cooked.

8. When the meatballs are done baking, transfer them to a large bowl and coat them in the sauce.

9. Serve and enjoy!

# WELCOME TO JAM ROCK

# BAKED JERK CHICKEN

**PREP TIME: 30 MINUTES (PLUS MARINATING OVERNIGHT) • COOK TIME: 1 HOUR 20 MINUTES**

When it comes to the most popular meal in Jamaica, that dish will always be jerk chicken. People travel from far and wide just to get their hands on this peppery and smoky succulent chicken. However, when prepared the traditional way on a coal smoker, it can take a considerable amount of time. Not only that, but not everyone owns a smoker. This oven-baked recipe is designed for anyone who loves the authentic taste of jerk chicken but just doesn't have the resources. This dish is a perfect 10/10, especially after being marinated overnight in your homemade jerk marinade. Try it out, serve it to your friends and family, and savor the authentic taste of Jamaica.

## Serves: 6–8

### FOR THE MARINADE

1 white or yellow onion, diced

3 whole Scotch bonnet or habanero peppers

Handful of green onions

2 tablespoons minced fresh ginger

10 sprigs of thyme

8 whole allspice berries

8 garlic cloves

Juice of 2 limes

3 tablespoons avocado oil

1 tablespoon light brown sugar

2 teaspoons browning sauce

1 tablespoon dark soy sauce

1 tablespoon kosher salt

1 teaspoon ground cinnamon

### FOR THE CHICKEN

6–8 chicken leg quarters

2 teaspoons garlic powder

2 teaspoons onion powder

½ tablespoon kosher salt

½ tablespoon freshly ground black pepper

1. To make the marinade, in a blender or large food processor, combine all the ingredients and blend on high until smooth.

2. Trim all the chicken quarters of excess fat and then score them vertically. (Scoring allows for a deeper marinade and crispier skin.)

3. Pat the chicken dry with paper towels and place them in a large bowl. Add the garlic powder, onion powder, salt, and black pepper. Add about 3–5 tablespoons of the marinade. Massage the seasonings evenly and under the skin. Cover and refrigerate overnight for best results.

4. Preheat the oven to 400°F (200°C).

5. Place the marinated chicken on an elevated baking rack and place in the oven to bake for 1 hour and 20 minutes, flipping halfway through.

6. Remove the chicken from the oven and allow it to rest for 10 minutes.

7. Serve with Jamaican Rice & Peas (page 72), Fried Ripe Plantains (page 73), and my Homemade Jerk BBQ Sauce (page 199).

# BROWN STEW CHICKEN

**PREP TIME: 30 MINUTES (PLUS MARINATING TIME) • COOK TIME: 1 HOUR 30 MINUTES**

Every Sunday after church growing up, my parents took turns making brown stew chicken. In fact, it was the first Jamaican dish I ever learned how to make. Every bite takes me back to a simpler time in my life, way before I was able to write a cookbook. The simplicity of this dish will always hold a special place in my heart. Delight in succulent chicken pieces, expertly marinated and slow-cooked in a delicious sauce infused with the flavors of Jamaica. For an even more delightful experience, pair it with a side of sweet Fried Ripe Plantains (see page 73) to complete your meal. There is no dish more comforting in our cuisine than this one. You have to try it!

## Serves: 4–6

2 lbs (907g) bone-in chicken thighs and legs (or use a whole young chicken broken down into 5 pieces, see tip)

1 tablespoon all-purpose seasoning

2 teaspoons smoked paprika

1 teaspoon ground allspice

1 teaspoon chicken bouillon powder

1 teaspoon garlic powder

1 teaspoon onion powder

2 teaspoons kosher salt

1 teaspoon freshly ground black pepper

2 teaspoons browning sauce, divided

2 tablespoons avocado oil

1½ cups chicken broth

1 yellow onion, chopped

4 garlic cloves, minced

1 red or green bell pepper, chopped

1 Scotch bonnet pepper or habanero pepper (optional), thinly sliced

6 sprigs of thyme

¼ cup ketchup

2 tablespoons soy sauce

1. In a large bowl, combine the chicken, all-purpose seasoning, smoked paprika, ground allspice, bouillon powder, garlic powder, onion powder, salt, and pepper, and 1 tablespoon of browning sauce. Mix well to coat. Cover and refrigerate to marinate for 2–24 hours.

2. To a Dutch oven over medium-high heat, add the avocado oil. Once hot, sear the chicken until it has a dark brown color to lock in the flavors.

3. Add the chicken broth and bring to a boil. Once at a boil, add the onion, garlic, bell pepper, Scotch bonnet pepper (if using), thyme, ketchup, soy sauce, and the remaining 1 tablespoon of browning sauce. Stir well and simmer for 40 minutes or until the chicken is cooked and tender.

4. Remove the Dutch oven from the heat. Serve with Jamaican Rice & Peas (page 72) or jasmine rice if you want to keep it simple.

**TIP:** To break the whole chicken down into pieces, use a sharp knife to separate the breasts, thighs, drums and wings. Then, break the thighs and breasts down into 4 chunks each and leave the legs and wings whole.

# JAMAICAN CURRY CHICKEN

**PREP TIME: 20 MINUTES • COOK TIME: 1 HOUR**

Every island in the Caribbean prepares curry differently, but if you're looking for a prominent, spicy flavor profile, Jamaican-style curry is exactly what you need. This dish always hits home for me because it was a staple in my upbringing—and my mother's rendition will always be the best no matter how many variations I try. I know I'm biased, but there's no shame in my game. The whole chicken cooked down with bones adds a deeper level of flavor after simmering in a pot for an hour with fresh herbs and aromatics. Serve it with jasmine or basmati rice and you'll have not only a hearty meal but also a healthy one.

## Serves: 4–6

1 whole chicken, sectioned into 5 pieces (see tip)

2 tablespoons Jamaican curry powder, divided

1 teaspoon ground turmeric

¼ teaspoon ground cumin

1 teaspoon garlic powder

1 teaspoon onion powder

2 teaspoons all-purpose seasoning, divided

1 teaspoon kosher salt

½ teaspoon freshly ground black pepper

2 tablespoons canola oil

5 garlic cloves, minced

5 whole allspice berries

1 green bell pepper, seeded and diced

5 sprigs of thyme

½ cup chopped green onions, white and green parts

1 white or yellow onion, diced

2 cups chicken stock or broth

1 tablespoon roasted chicken base

2 russet potatoes, peeled and finely cubed

1. In a large bowl, combine the chicken, 1 tablespoon of curry powder, turmeric, cumin, garlic powder, onion powder, 1 teaspoon of all-purpose seasoning, and salt and pepper. Mix well to coat.

2. To a Dutch oven or large pot over medium heat, add the canola oil. Once hot, add the remaining curry powder and toast for 2–3 minutes, until fragrant. Add the chicken and cook for 8 minutes, flipping occasionally until seared.

3. Add the garlic, whole allspice berries, bell pepper, thyme, green onion, and onion. Stir in the chicken stock and roasted chicken base. Bring to a boil.

4. Once at a boil, reduce the heat to low and simmer for 45 minutes. Add the potatoes along with the remaining teaspoon of all-purpose seasoning and cook for 15 minutes more or until the potatoes are soft.

5. Taste the broth and season to taste.

6. Remove the Dutch oven from the heat and serve with white rice or roti.

**TIP:** To break the whole chicken down into pieces, use a sharp knife to separate the breasts, thighs, drums and wings. Then, break the thighs and breasts down into 4 chunks each and leave the legs and wings whole.

# BEEF PATTIES

**PREP TIME: 1 HOUR (PLUS REFRIGERATION TIME) • COOK TIME: 30 MINUTES**

Much like pizza is to the working class in New York City, our casual meal on the go in Jamaica is the famous patty, most famously the beef patty. Encased in buttery dough, these spicy beef patties never seems to get old, no matter how many times I visit home and order them. While they can be a task to make, they are worth it every time. Just grab some friends, man your station, and get to cooking!

## Makes: 8 patties, depending on size

### FOR THE PATTY DOUGH

2 cups all-purpose flour, plus more

1 teaspoon kosher salt

½ teaspoon ground turmeric

¼ teaspoon Jamaican curry powder

½ cup cold and grated unsalted butter

2 egg yolks, beaten

### FOR THE FILLING

1 tablespoon avocado oil

1lb (454g) ground beef

1 white or yellow onion, finely diced

4 garlic cloves, minced

2 teaspoons dried thyme leaves

¼ teaspoon ground allspice

1 teaspoon Jamaican curry powder

¼ teaspoon ground cumin

1 Scotch bonnet or habanero pepper, diced

2 green onions, green parts only, finely chopped

Kosher salt and freshly ground black pepper, to taste

¼ cup breadcrumbs

¼ cup chicken broth

1. Preheat the oven to 400°F (200°C).

2. To make the patty dough, in a large bowl, whisk together the flour, salt, turmeric, and curry powder.

3. Add the grated butter and use a pastry cutter to mix it into the flour mixture. Gradually add up to a ¼ cup water while mixing with until a dough ball is formed.

4. On a floured counter or clean surface, knead the dough until smooth. Wrap the dough with plastic wrap and refrigerate for 30 minutes.

5. To make the filling, in a medium skillet over medium heat, add the avocado oil. Once hot, add the ground beef and brown until fully cooked. Drain any excess liquid or fat for best results.

6. Stir in the onion, garlic, thyme, allspice, curry powder, cumin, Scotch bonnet pepper, and green onions. Cook until the onions and garlic are soft and fragrant, about 2 minutes.

Season with salt and pepper to taste.

7. Add the breadcrumbs and chicken broth. Cook until the beef filling is thick and gravy-like.

8. Place the patty dough on a floured surface. Use a rolling pin to roll out the dough to about ⅛ inch (3mm) thick. Use a pizza cutter or a cookie cutter to cut the dough into circles.

9. Place a spoonful of the beef filling in the center of the dough, fold the edges in half, brush the edges with egg wash, and use a fork to crimp the edges.

10. Line a baking sheet with parchment paper and evenly place the patties on the sheet. Brush each patty with egg wash.

11. Place the sheet in the oven and bake for 30 minutes or until the patties are golden brown.

12. Serve hot—and prepare to clean the crumbs off your lap!

# CARIBBEAN-STYLE PEPPER STEAK

**PREP TIME: 15 MINUTES (PLUS MARINATING OVERNIGHT) • COOK TIME: 15 MINUTES**

While not the most traditional, pepper steak was one of my favorites to get from the cafeteria during my time going to school in Jamaica. It's a flavorful but spicy dish made with a lean but very tender steak cut; marinated to perfection in garlic, ginger, and soy sauce; and stir-fried with onions and peppers. It's so simple to make but captures such an amazing flavor profile that you can eat it with any side. It also serves as an amazing meal prep dish for those who are always on the go.

## Serves: 4

2 lbs (907g) flank steak, cut thinly across the grain

1 teaspoon adobo

1 teaspoon Easispice Meat Seasoning

1 teaspoon soy sauce

1 tablespoon minced ginger, divided

2 tablespoons minced garlic, divided

4 tablespoons avocado oil, divided

½ white or yellow onion, thinly sliced

½ green bell pepper, seeded and thinly sliced

½ yellow bell pepper, seeded and thinly sliced

½ red bell pepper, seeded and thinly sliced

2 cups beef broth

1 teaspoon browning sauce

5 sprigs of thyme

1 Scotch bonnet or habanero pepper, chopped

¼ cup chopped green onion, white and green parts

5 whole allspice berries

3 tablespoons cornstarch

1. In a large bowl, combine the flank steak, adobo, Easispice Meat Seasoning, soy sauce, ½ tablespoon of ginger, and 1 tablespoon of garlic. Cover and refrigerate overnight to marinate.

2. To a large skillet over medium heat, add 3 tablespoons of avocado oil. Once hot, add the steak and cook 80% through (the pieces will just start to curl up at this point). Remove the steak from the skillet and set aside.

3. Add the remaining 1 tablespoon of avocado oil to the same skillet. Add the onion and sauté for 30 seconds. Add the bell peppers and sauté for 30 seconds more.

4. Once the peppers and onions are partially soft, add the remaining ½ tablespoon of ginger and the remaining 1 tablespoon of garlic. Stir continuously to prevent them from burning.

5. Add the cooked flank steak and stir in the beef broth, browning sauce, thyme, Scotch bonnet pepper, green onion, and whole allspice berries. Bring to a simmer for 5 minutes.

6. In a small dish, combine the cornstarch and 6 tablespoons of water to create a slurry. Add this to the skillet and cook until the sauce begins to thicken, stirring occasionally.

7. Transfer everything to a serving platter and enjoy!

# OXTAIL

**PREP TIME: 30 MINUTES (PLUS MARINATING TIME) • COOK TIME: 2 HOURS 30 MINUTES**

Do you want tender, fall-off-the-bone oxtail every time you make it? Then this is the recipe you need to follow. Out of every dish I grew up eating, oxtail is the one that never gets old. This dish is a flavor masterpiece with oxtail braising in a combination of aromatics, spices, and herbs. Braise it low and slow for the best results, and serve it with Jamaican Rice & Peas (page 72) for an amazing plate you'll never forget!

## Serves: 4–6

3 lbs (1.4kg) oxtail, excess fat around the edges trimmed if necessary

2 teaspoons seasoned salt, divided

2 teaspoons garlic powder, divided

2 teaspoons onion powder, divided

1 teaspoon freshly ground black pepper

1 teaspoon soy sauce

1 teaspoon complete seasoning

2 teaspoons browning sauce, divided

3 tablespoons avocado oil

2 tablespoons minced garlic

6 sprigs of thyme

½ white or yellow onion, sliced

½ red bell pepper, sliced

2 teaspoons all-purpose seasoning

2 Scotch bonnet or habanero peppers, left whole or cut in half

1 (8oz [227g]) can of butter beans, drained

1. In a large bowl, combine the oxtail, 1 teaspoon of seasoned salt, 1 teaspoon of garlic powder, 1 teaspoon of onion powder, black pepper, soy sauce, the complete seasoning, and 1 teapoon of browning sauce. Cover and refrigerate to marinate for 2–24 hours.

2. To a Dutch oven over medium heat, add the avocado oil. Once hot, add the oxtail and brown for 3 minutes on both sides.

3. Transfer the oxtail to a pressure cooker and pressure cook on high for 30 minutes.

4. Transfer the oxtail back to the Dutch oven and add enough water to barely cover the oxtail.

5. Add the minced garlic, thyme, onion, bell pepper, Scotch bonnet pepper (if using), the all-purpose seasoning, the remaining teaspoon of the garlic powder, the remaining teaspoon of the onion powder, the remaining teaspoon of the seasoned salt, and the remaining teaspoon of the browning sauce. Bring to a boil over medium heat.

6. Once at a boil, reduce the heat to medium-low and allow to stew for 1–2 hours depending on how tender you want your final product. Before the last 10 minutes of cooking, add the butter beans.

7. Remove the Dutch oven from the heat and serve immediately.

# PHILLIP'S FAMOUS CURRY GOAT

**PREP TIME: 20 MINUTES (PLUS MARINATING OVERNIGHT) • COOK TIME: 2–3 HOURS**

Goat meat is a delicacy in Jamaica, so if you're tasked with making curry goat for a family gathering, you better do it right. This recipe is my father's, and it will get the job done every time. The meat is cooked with Jamaican curry powder, thyme, and ginger, and a Scotch bonnet pepper. Potatoes are added to give you extra carbs for a thick gravy to pour over Jamaican Rice & Peas (page 72). While goat isn't commonly eaten in every culture, try it once and you'll be hooked for life.

## Serves: 4–6

2 lbs (907g) bone-in goat meat, cut into small chunks

2 tablespoons Jamaican curry powder, divided

2 teaspoons ground turmeric, divided

2 teaspoons ground cumin, divided

2 teaspoons garlic powder

2 teaspoons onion powder

kosher salt and black pepper, to taste

2 tablespoons canola oil

1 sweet onion, diced

4 garlic cloves, minced

½ tablespoon minced fresh ginger

½ green bell pepper, seeded and diced

6 green onions, white and green parts, finely chopped

1 whole Scotch bonnet pepper or habanero pepper

3–5 sprigs of thyme

½ tablespoon roasted chicken base

2 russet potatoes, peeled and cubed into bite-sized pieces

1. In a large bowl, combine the goat meat, 1 tablespoon of curry powder, 1 teaspoon turmeric, 1 teaspoon cumin, garlic powder, onion powder, and salt and pepper to taste. Rub the spices in with your hands. Cover and refrigerate overnight to marinate.

2. To a large pot or Dutch oven over medium heat, add the canola oil. Once hot, add the remaining 1 tablespoon of curry powder, the remaining 1 teaspoon of turmeric, and the remaining 1 teaspoon of cumin. Cook until the spices become fragrant.

3. Add the goat meat and cook until browned on all sides, about 8 minutes.

4. Add the sweet onion, garlic, ginger, bell pepper, green onions, Scotch bonnet pepper, and thyme. Stir in 2 cups of water and the roasted chicken base. Bring to a boil.

5. Once at a boil, reduce the heat to low, cover the pot, and simmer for 2–3 hours.

6. Add the potatoes to the pot and simmer until they're cooked through.

7. Remove the Dutch oven from the heat and serve with Jamaican Rice & Peas (page 72) and Fried Ripe Plantains (page 73).

# JERK SALMON FILLETS

**PREP TIME: 15 MINUTES (PLUS MARINATING TIME) • COOK TIME: 20 MINUTES**

This recipe is for my pescatarian friends who want to enjoy the bold flavors of Jamaican jerk chicken. With this recipe, I give your same old salmon a fabulous twist by marinating it in homemade jerk seasoning and baking it to perfection. The result is a mouthwatering salmon fillet bursting with spicy flavors. This dish is not only delicious but also easy to make—perfect for cooks of all levels. Give it a try and let me know what you think!

## Makes: 4 fillets

### FOR THE MARINADE

1 white or yellow onion, diced

3 whole Scotch bonnet or
    habanero peppers

Handful of green onions,
    roughly chopped

2 tablespoons minced fresh
    ginger

10 sprigs of thyme

8 whole allspice berries

8 garlic cloves

Juice of 2 limes

3 tablespoons avocado oil

1 tablespoon light brown sugar

2 teaspoons browning sauce

1 tablespoon dark soy sauce

1 tablespoon kosher salt

1 teaspoon cinnamon

### FOR THE FILLETS

4 salmon fillets, about 1lb
    (454g) total

Kosher salt and freshly ground
    black pepper, to taste

1. Place the salmon on a baking sheet. Season with salt and pepper to taste. Rub the seasonings in well.

2. In a large food processor or blender, blend all the marinade ingredients on high.

3. Pour the marinade over the salmon and rub the mixture in. Cover and refrigerate to marinate for 1–2 hours.

4. Preheat the oven to 400°F (200°C).

5. Place the salmon on an elevated baking rack in the oven and bake for 20–25 minutes or until the salmon easily comes apart with a fork.

6. Serve hot with roasted vegetables or Jamaican Rice & Peas (page 72).

# CURRY LOBSTER TAILS

**PREP TIME: 15 MINUTES • COOK TIME: 15 MINUTES**

Curry lobster tail is a delicious and flavor-packed seafood dish that's perfect for any occasion. The delicate lobster meat is stewed in a creamy coconut curry sauce that's infused with traditional Jamaican curry and our staple herbs and aromatics, taking the overall flavor to new heights. Add the Scotch bonnet pepper if you love heat, or leave it out for a sweeter and subtler bite. This recipe doesn't take long to make, but it will impress anyone you need to in a short amount of time.

## Serves: 4

2 tablespoons canola oil

½ yellow onion, diced

4 garlic cloves, minced

½ tablespoon minced fresh ginger

1 Scotch bonnet or habanero pepper, minced

1½ tablespoon Jamaican curry powder

1 teaspoon ground allspice

½ teaspoon ground cumin

1 teaspoon ground paprika

½ teaspoon garlic powder

½ teaspoon onion powder

1½ teaspoon kosher salt, plus more

½ teaspoon freshly ground black pepper, plus more

2 sprigs of thyme

1 cup coconut milk

4 lobster tails (1lb [454g] total), meat removed from the shell, cleaned, deveined, and cut into bite-sized pieces (see tip)

Cooked white rice or 1 batch Festival Dumplings (page 70), for serving

1. To a large skillet or saucepan over medium heat, add the canola oil. Once hot, sauté the onion, garlic, ginger, and Scotch bonnet pepper until soft and fragrant.

2. Add the curry powder, allspice, cumin, paprika, garlic powder, onion powder, salt, and pepper. Cook until the spices become fragrant, about 2 minutes.

3. Stir in the coconut milk and thyme. Bring the mixture to a simmer and allow to cook for 3–5 minutes.

4. Add the lobster meat and stir until coated. Cover and cook for 5–10 minutes until the lobster is cooked through. Season with salt and black pepper to taste.

5. Serve with white rice or Festival Dumplings (page 70).

**TIP:** To remove lobster meat from the shell, use kitchen scissors to carefully cut along the soft underside of the tail. Lift the meat gently, keeping it attached at the narrow end, and then place it on top of the shell.

# FESTIVAL DUMPLINGS

**PREP TIME: 10-15 MINUTES • COOK TIME: ABOUT 15 MINUTES**

Festival dumplings are a very popular street food in Jamaica, most commonly enjoyed with fried fish at the seaside. These dumplings are prepared with a mixture of flour, cornmeal, and a hint of sugar to add the perfect amount of sweetness! Then they're fried to perfection, leaving you with a crunchy exterior and a soft and light interior. While festival dumplings are commonly served at dinner, try them as an appetizer with your favorite dip for a tasty treat.

## Makes: 10 dumplings

2 cups all-purpose flour, plus more

¼ cup cornmeal

2 tablespoons granulated sugar

2 teaspoons baking powder

1 teaspoon kosher salt

½ teaspoon ground nutmeg

½ cup coconut milk

Vegetable oil, for frying

1. In a large bowl, whisk together the flour, cornmeal, sugar, baking powder, salt, and nutmeg.

2. In a small bowl, whisk together ½ cup water and the coconut milk.

3. Slowly pour the liquid ingredients into the dry ingredients, mixing with your hands until a dough forms.

4. On a floured counter or clean surface, knead the dough until smooth. Rip the dough into 10 portions and roll them into thick cylinders.

5. To a large Dutch oven or pot over medium heat, add 3–4 inches (7.5 to 10cm) of vegetable oil and heat to 350°F (180°C).

6. Once hot, working in small batches, add the dumplings and fry for 5 minutes or until golden brown.

7. Transfer the dumplings to an elevated wire rack to drain the excess oil.

8. Serve hot and enjoy.

# JAMAICAN RICE & PEAS

**PREP TIME: 10 MINUTES (PLUS SOAKING OVERNIGHT) • COOK TIME: 1 HOUR**

When talking about a staple dish in Jamaican culture, the one that rules supreme is—hands down—rice and peas. We eat it with everything! The dish is so simple and pairs well with almost every Jamaican dish I've created in this cookbook. It's a simple combination of kidney beans, rice, and coconut milk, along with staple spices from Jamaican cuisine. Pair it with extra gravy for the full effect and a perfect spoonful.

## Serves: 6

1 cup of dried red kidney beans, soaked overnight and drained

1 (13.5oz [400ml]) can of coconut milk

3 garlic cloves

3 sprigs of thyme

3 green onions, chopped, green parts only

5 whole allspice berries

1 Scotch bonnet or habanero pepper (optional)

Kosher salt and freshly ground black pepper, to taste

2 cups basmati rice, washed

1. Add the drained kidney beans to a large pot and cover with 4 cups of water.

2. Stir in the coconut milk, garlic, thyme, green onions, allspice berries, Scotch bonnet pepper (if using), and salt and pepper to taste. Mix well and bring to a boil over high heat.

3. Once at a boil, reduce the heat to low and simmer for 20–30 minutes or until the beans are tender.

4. Add the rice and 2 cups of water and mix to combine. Increase the heat to medium-high and bring everything to a boil again.

5. Once at a boil, reduce the heat to low and cover the pot with a tight-fitting lid. Simmer for 20–30 minutes or until the rice is fluffy.

6. Transfer everything to a serving dish and enjoy as a side dish with many of the Jamaican staples I've offered in this book.

# FRIED RIPE PLANTAINS

**PREP TIME: 10 MINUTES • COOK TIME: 10 MINUTES**

Fried ripe plantains are a popular side dish in many Caribbean countries and are a delicious treat that is actually very easy to make. They are made by pan-frying sliced ripe plantains until caramelized on the inside and crispy on the outside. Serve them by themselves or as a side with brown stew, jerk, and even curry chicken for an amazing pairing.

## Serves: 2–4

2 ripe plantains
3 tablespoons canola oil
Kosher salt, to taste

1. Peel the plantains by cutting them lengthwise and use your fingers to open and completely peel off the skin. Slice the plantains into ½-inch-thick (1.25cm) circles.

2. To a medium skillet over medium heat, add the canola oil. Once hot, fry the plantains on each side until golden brown.

3. Transfer the plantains to a bowl lined with paper towels to soak up the excess oil. Sprinkle salt, to taste, over the top while still warm.

4. Serve and enjoy.

# STEAMED CABBAGE & CARROTS

**PREP TIME: 15 MINUTES • COOK TIME: 20 MINUTES**

What's a Jamaican dinner without a side of steamed cabbage? Including this dish in a Jamaican meal will infuse your family table with the vibrant flavors of the Caribbean. Thinly shredded cabbage is mixed with carrots and fragrant aromatics, such as fresh garlic and ground allspice, then simmered together to create a simple and delicious treat. Serve it alongside jerk chicken, curry goat, or any other Jamaican dish, and take a seat at the family table to savor the authentic taste of Jamaica.

## Serves: 4–6

2 tablespoons canola oil

1 yellow onion, diced

5 garlic cloves, minced

1 large cabbage, shredded

3 large carrots, shredded

¼ teaspoon ground allspice

½ teaspoon dried thyme leaves

1 teaspoon garlic powder

Kosher salt and freshly ground black pepper, to taste

1. In a large skillet over medium heat, add the canola oil. Once hot, add the onions and garlic, and sauté until soft and fragrant.

2. Add the cabbage, carrots, allspice, thyme, garlic powder, and salt and pepper to taste. Mix until well combined.

3. Add a ¼ cup of water, cover with an airtight lid, and simmer for 15 minutes or until the cabbage is soft and tender. Occasionally remove the lid to let any excess water evaporate.

4. Serve hot as a side at dinner and enjoy.

# SWEET MACARONI SALAD

**PREP TIME: 20 MINUTES • COOK TIME: 10-12 MINUTES**

In Jamaica, we serve dinner with very few sides, but one side you'll commonly find at small restaurants throughout the island is macaroni salad. The creamy mayonnaise-based dressing is complemented so well with vinegar and sugar, creating a savory but also sweet side dish you can pair with almost every protein for dinner. Always remember to make it ahead of time so it's nice and chilled come dinnertime. Not only is it better served cold, but it also allows the flavors to meld together!

## Serves: 4–6

1lb (454g) elbow macaroni

1 cup mayonnaise

1 tablespoon white vinegar

2 tablespoons sweetened
   condensed milk

1 tablespoon granulated sugar

¼ cup finely diced yellow onion

¼ cup finely diced green
   bell pepper

¼ cup finely diced red
   bell pepper

1 teaspoon dried thyme leaves

¼ cup finely diced celery

3 medium carrots, grated

Kosher salt and freshly ground
   black pepper, to taste

1. Cook the macaroni according to package instructions. Drain and rinse the macaroni and set aside to cool slightly.

2. In a large bowl, combine the mayonnaise, white vinegar, condensed milk, sugar, onion, bell peppers, thyme, celery, and carrots. Mix well.

3. Once the macaroni is warm, not hot, add it to the bowl with the dressing and mix until everything is well combined. Add the salt and black pepper to taste.

4. Cover with plastic wrap and refrigerate for 1 hour before serving.

# SOUL-FILLED HOLIDAY SEASON

# FIVE CHEESE MAC & CHEESE, MY WAY

**PREP TIME: 25 MINUTES • COOK TIME: 25 MINUTES (PLUS COOLING TIME)**

Mac and cheese is a favorite dish, but let's be real: If you don't get it right, you might never be trusted with making it for the family gathering ever again. Fear not, because this recipe is certified to have you on mac and cheese duty for a lifetime. Get ready for a creamy, cheesy delight that will leave everyone begging for more. With perfectly cooked, tender elbow noodles and a rich cheese sauce featuring sharp cheddar, mozzarella, Gruyère, smoked gouda, and Colby-Jack cheeses, along with a blend of spices and a touch of cream cheese for added flavor, this recipe is sure to satisfy the cheese lovers in the family.

## Serves: 6–8

2 teaspoons kosher salt, plus more

6 cups large elbow macaroni

8 tablespoons unsalted butter

3 tablespoons all-purpose flour

½ tablespoon onion powder

½ tablespoon garlic powder

½ tablespoon smoked paprika

3 cups heavy cream

8 ounces (227g) shredded sharp cheddar cheese, divided

8 ounces (227g) shredded Gruyère cheese, divided

8 ounces (227g) shredded mozzarella, divided

8 ounces (227g) shredded smoked Gouda cheese, divided

8 ounces (227g) shredded Colby-jack cheese, divided

1 tablespoon cream cheese

Freshly ground black pepper, to taste

**TIP:** When someone says "your sauce broke," it means your sauce has separated into its components, losing its smooth texture. This can happen to cheese sauces, mayonnaise-based sauces, and custards. For example: in cheese sauces, the fats (butter and cheese) separate from the liquid (usually milk) when the sauce is heated too quickly or at too high a temperature.

1. Preheat the oven to 350°F (180°C).

2. To a large pot over medium heat, add 10 cups of water and a pinch of salt. Bring to a boil.

3. Once at a boil, add the elbow macaroni and cook until cook until al dente.

4. Drain the water and cover the pasta fully in cold water. Repeat until the pasta is at room temperature. Set aside.

5. In a large skillet over low heat, add the butter.

6. Once the butter is melted, whisk in the flour to make a roux. Whisk until the flour is fully dissolved.

7. Whisk in the onion powder, garlic powder, smoked paprika, and salt. Whisk until everything is well incorporated.

8. Whisk in the heavy cream. Once the sauce starts to bubble, completely turn off the heat. (This prevents the sauce from breaking. See tip.)

9. Whisk in ½ cup each of the sharp Cheddar, mozzarella, Gruyère, Gouda, and Colby-Jack cheeses. Continue whisking while adding the cream cheese and black pepper.

10. Add the cooked pasta and mix evenly. Pour the mixture into a 9 × 13-inch (23 × 33cm) baking dish and top with the remaining cheese.

11. Place the dish in the oven and bake for 25 minutes or until the mac and cheese reaches your desired color.

12. Remove the dish from the oven and allow the mac and cheese to cool for 25 minutes before serving.

# GRANDMA'S CORN BREAD

**PREP TIME: 5–10 MINUTES • COOK TIME: 25 MINUTES**

I call this recipe "Grandma's Corn Bread" because it's a taste of home that's perfect for any holiday get-together. Corn bread is a Southern classic that is filled with love and will warm you right up. Baked in a cast-iron skillet, this corn bread possesses a crispy crust with a soft and buttery interior that's to die for. The honey butter then adds the perfect amount of moisture and sweetness, making the combo the most comforting dish. Eat it as a side or crush it up and use it in my Corn Bread Dressing recipe (page 85). This corn bread is meant to turn heads and I can almost guarantee it will be a favorite among your friends and family!

## Serves: 8–12

1½ cups all-purpose flour

1½ cups cornmeal

⅔ cup white granulated sugar

1 teaspoon kosher salt

3½ teaspoons baking powder

½ cup melted butter

1 large egg

1½ cups buttermilk

1. Preheat the oven to 400°F (200°C). Grease a 9-inch (23cm) cast-iron skillet or baking dish.

2. In a medium bowl, whisk together the flour, cornmeal, sugar, salt, and baking powder.

3. Add the melted butter, egg, and buttermilk. Whisk until fully incorporated. Pour the batter into the greased skillet.

4. Place the skillet in the oven and bake for 25 minutes.

5. Serve warm or let sit for 3 hours if you're using the corn bread to make my Corn Bread Dressing (page 85).

# CORN BREAD DRESSING

**PREP TIME: 35 MINUTES • COOK TIME: 2 HOURS 45 MINUTES**

Embrace the warmth of homemade greatness with this classic holiday side. This corn bread dressing is bursting with flavors and herbs and is truly a comforting staple on any dinner table. The mix of flavorful chicken, sautéed vegetables, and corn bread comes together to create harmony. Add this recipe to your list of staples and you won't be disappointed.

## Serves: 6–8

5 tablespoons poultry seasoning, divided

2 tablespoons roasted chicken base

5 sprigs of thyme

5 sprigs of parsley

2 sprigs of rosemary

5 garlic cloves

2 white or yellow onions: 1 diced; 1 whole

1 red bell pepper: ½ diced; ½ whole

1 green bell pepper: ½ diced; ½ whole

6 celery stalks: 3 diced; 3 whole

1 dried bay leaf

1½ lbs (680g) bone-in chicken breasts or thighs

1 batch Grandma's Corn Bread (see page 82)

2 tablespoons minced garlic

3 tablespoons minced fresh sage

8 tablespoons unsalted butter

1 large egg

4 cups homemade chicken stock (made within this recipe)

1 (10oz [285g]) can of cream of chicken soup

1. To a large pot over high heat, add 10 cups of water. Bring to a boil, then add 3 tablespoons of the poultry seasoning, the chicken base, thyme, parsley, rosemary, garlic, whole onion, ½ whole red bell pepper, ½ whole green bell pepper, 3 whole celery stalks, bay leaf, and chicken. Boil for 2 hours.

2. Preheat the oven to 375°F (190°C). Grease a 9 × 13-inch (23 × 33cm) baking dish.

3. Remove the chicken from the broth, remove the skin, shred, and debone. Place the chicken in a large bowl and set aside. Strain the chicken broth and reserve the clarified liquid.

4. Crumble the corn bread into a large bowl. Set aside.

5. To a large skillet over medium heat, add the butter. Once melted, add the diced onion, ½ diced red bell pepper, ½ diced green bell pepper, 3 diced celery stalks, garlic, sage, and 1 tablespoon of the poultry seasoning. Sauté the vegetables for 2–3 minutes.

6. Add everything in the skillet to the corn bread. Stir in the egg, cream of chicken soup, shredded chicken, and the remaining 1 tablespoon of poultry seasoning. Slowly stir in the chicken stock until the mixture reaches your desired texture. Add the mixture to the prepared baking dish.

7. Place the dish in the oven and bake for 45 minutes.

8. Remove the dish from the oven and allow the dressing to cool for 20 minutes before serving.

# SWEET CITRUS-GLAZED HAM

**PREP TIME: 20 MINUTES • COOK TIME: 2 HOURS 20 MINUTES**

What's a holiday without a ham? This beautiful dinner centerpiece is perfect for any special occasion. A 10-pound (4.5kg) spiral ham is bathed in a rich combination of melted butter, pineapple juice, and just a touch of liquid smoke. This combination created a tender and juicy ham that's then glazed with a blend of brown sugar, orange marmalade, Dijon mustard, and aromatic spices. Each slice of this tender ham is irresistible and will elevate every gathering, creating lasting memories.

## Serves: 10–15

### FOR THE HAM

10 lb (4.5kg) spiral ham

4 tablespoons unsalted butter, melted

2 cups pineapple juice

½ cup liquid smoke

### FOR THE GLAZE

8 tablespoons unsalted butter

1 cup light brown sugar

½ cup hot honey

½ cup honey

½ cup orange marmalade

2 tablespoons Dijon mustard

1 tablespoon balsamic vinegar

1 tablespoon ginger paste

1 teaspoon ground cinnamon

1 teaspoon ground nutmeg

1 teaspoon ground cloves

1. Preheat the oven to 325°F (165°C). Place the ham in a 9 × 13-inch (23 × 33cm) aluminum foil baking pan.

2. In a small bowl, combine the butter, pineapple juice, and liquid smoke. Mix well. Pour over the ham and tightly cover the pan with aluminum foil.

3. Place the pan in the oven and bake for 2 hours.

4. To make the glaze, in a medium skillet over low heat, combine all the ingredients. Stir frequently for about 10 minutes, or until the glaze reaches a syrupy texture.

5. Remove the ham from the oven and increase the oven temperature to 425°F (220°C). Generously coat the ham with the glaze, making sure to get between each slice.

6. Return the pan to the oven and bake uncovered for 20 minutes, basting every 5 minutes.

7. Remove the pan from the oven and allow the ham to rest for 20 minutes before serving.

# SMOTHERED TURKEY WINGS

**PREP TIME: 25 MINUTES • COOK TIME: 2 HOURS 15 MINUTES**

Not a fan of the same old dry, oven-baked turkey? Then give these smothered turkey wings a try! They are the perfect comfort meal for any day of the week and are a great addition to everyone's holiday spread. The wings are seasoned to perfection with a blend of spices, then baked with fresh cut peppers and onions for extra aroma. To set them off even further, they are coated in a thick gravy made with chicken stock, sage, and red pepper flakes for a delicious finish. This recipe is easy to make and perfect for feeding a hungry crowd. Be sure to give it a try.

## Serves: 4

4 tablespoons unsalted butter

1 onion, sliced, divided

2 tablespoons minced garlic

1 tablespoon fresh sage

1 tablespoon roasted chicken base

1 teaspoon plus 1 tablespoon smoked paprika, divided

3 tablespoons all-purpose flour

3 cups low-sodium chicken stock

½ tablespoon crushed red pepper flakes (optional)

kosher salt and freshly ground black pepper, to taste

4 turkey wings, unseparated

3 tablespoons avocado oil

½ tablespoon chili powder

1 tablespoon oregano

1 tablespoon onion powder

1 tablespoon garlic powder

½ red bell pepper, julienned

½ green bell pepper, julienned

1. Preheat the oven to 375°F (190°C).

2. To a medium nonstick skillet over medium heat, add the butter. Once melted, add ½ the onion as well as the garlic and sage. Sauté until fragrant.

3. Whisk in the roasted chicken base and 1 teaspoon of paprika. Stir in the flour until it dissolves.

4. Stir in the chicken stock. Add the red pepper flakes (if using) and salt and black pepper to taste. Remove the skillet from the heat and set aside.

5. Separate the drumettes from the flats of the turkey wings. When this step is done, you should have 8 wings.

6. In a 9 × 13-inch (23 × 33cm) baking dish, combine the wings, avocado oil, chili powder, oregano, onion powder, garlic powder, and the remaining 1 tablespoon of paprika. Massage the seasonings into the wings.

7. Cover the wings with the bell peppers and the remaining ½ onion. Cover the dish with aluminum foil and place in the oven for 90 minutes.

8. Once done with its first bake, uncover and coat in the gravy. Bake uncovered for 45 minutes more.

9. Serve and enjoy.

# SOUTHERN FRIED CABBAGE

**PREP TIME: 10–15 MINUTES • COOK TIME: 10–15 MINUTES**

Looking for a delicious and flavorful green side dish? Try this Southern fried cabbage recipe, featuring thinly sliced cabbage sautéed with crispy bacon and smoked andouille sausage for the perfect spicy kick. The dish is enhanced with a variety of bell peppers, making it not only tasty but also nutritious. Plus, it's perfect for the keto lovers out there. Give it a try and let me know what you think!

## Serves: 4–6 people

4 thick-cut bacon strips

2 tablespoons minced garlic

4 andouille sausage links, sliced

½ green bell pepper, julienned

½ red bell pepper, julienned

½ white or yellow onion, thinly sliced

1½ lbs (680g) cabbage, thinly sliced

1 tablespoon Cajun seasoning

2 tablespoons unsalted butter

1. To a large skillet over medium heat, add the bacon and cook until crispy. Transfer the bacon to a small bowl, leaving the bacon fat in the skillet.

2. Add the bell peppers and onions to the skillet, and sauté until soft.

3. Add the garlic and sauté for 30 seconds more or until fragrant.

4. Add the andouille sausages and brown for 3 minutes.

5. Once the sausage begins to brown, add the cabbage. Toss until the cabbage starts to wilt, then add the Cajun seasoning.

6. Add the butter, toss, then cover the skillet until the cabbage reaches the desired texture, about 15 minutes.

7. Crumble the reserved bacon and add it to the skillet, then mix to combine. Remove the skillet from the heat.

8. Serve and enjoy!

# SMOKED TURKEY & COLLARD GREENS

**PREP TIME: 30 MINUTES • COOK TIME: 2 HOURS 15 MINUTES**

Experience the Southern flavors we all know and love with this collard greens recipe. These greens are steamed to perfection with the addition of smoked turkey legs and an exquisite blend of flavors. This is the perfect pair for all your Southern dishes.

## Serves: 6–8 people

4 lb (1.8kg) collard greens chiffonade

1 tablespoon kosher salt, plus more

¾ cup distilled white vinegar

2 tablespoons avocado oil

1 white or yellow onion, julienned

2 tablespoons minced garlic

1 tomato, diced

3 cups beef broth

2 tablespoons roasted beef base

1 tablespoon crushed red pepper flakes

2½ lb smoked turkey leg

2 teaspoons adobo seasoning

1. In a large bowl, combine the collard greens, salt, and vinegar and cover with enough water to submerge everything fully. Allow to soak for 30 minutes. Drain and set aside.

2. To deep pot over medium heat, add the avocado oil. Once hot, add the onion and sauté until fragrant. Add garlic and tomato, and sauté for 30 seconds more.

3. Stir in the beef broth. Bring to a simmer, then stir in the Better Than Bouillon roast beef flavoring and red pepper flakes.

4. Add the turkey leg, cover, and cook for 45 minutes to 1 hour. Once the turkey starts to soften remove it from the pot, discard the skin and bone, then use a fork to tear the meat apart.

5. Add the collard greens, but **DON'T STIR**.

6. Reduce the heat to low, cover, and cook for 1 hour more. Stir in the adobo and use a fork to further shred the turkey meat to your desired size.

7. Season with salt to taste and serve.

# HERTHA'S POTATO SALAD

**PREP TIME: 20 MINUTES • COOK TIME: 20 MINUTES**

I cherish this recipe that's very close to my heart. For those who don't know, Hertha is my mother—and her potato salad is the best. It's a certified family favorite that has to be made for every gathering, delivering a cold bite of nostalgia every time. With simple yet flavorful ingredients like russet potatoes, chopped eggs, mayonnaise, hot dog relish, green onions, yellow onions, and fresh dill, this dish is an amazing blend of flavors and textures. Prepare it with care and attention because this recipe is a testament to the love and core memories shared between a mother and her child. Love you, Mom!

## Serves: 6–8

1½ teaspoons kosher salt, plus more

2½ lbs (1.1kg) russet potatoes, peeled and cubed (see tip)

4 large eggs

1 cup mayonnaise

½ cup pickle relish

4 green onions

½ yellow onion, diced

1 tablespoon chopped fresh dill

1½ teaspoons garlic powder

1½ teaspoons onion powder

Freshly ground black pepper, to taste

1. To a large pot over medium-high heat, add 12 cups of water and bring to boil. Add a few pinches of salt and the potatoes. Once the potatoes become fork-tender, drain and cover in cold water to stop the cooking process.

2. Fill a medium pot a third of the way with water and place over medium-high heat. Once at a boil, place the eggs gently into the water and boil for 10 minutes. Carefully remove the eggs from the pot and allow them to slightly cool. Peel the eggs then finely chop them. Set aside.

3. In a large bowl, combine the mayonnaise, relish, green onions, yellow onion, and dill. Mix well.

4. Add the potatoes, eggs, salt, garlic powder, and onion powder. Stir until the potatoes and eggs are well coated with the dressing. Season with salt and pepper to taste.

5. Refrigerate for a few hours before serving.

**TIP:** Soak the peeled potatoes in cold water while waiting for the pot to boil so the potatoes don't begin to brown.

# SWEET CANDIED YAMS

**PREP TIME: 10–15 MINUTES • COOK TIME: 1 HOUR 15 MINUTES**

When in need of a tasty and sweet side dish at your next family gathering, look no further than these candied yams. With the perfect blend of sugar and spice, this a dream come true for any person with a sweet tooth. I added just a touch of maple syrup and ginger paste for a hearty flavor you won't forget. This dish is super satisfying, with the most tender and tasty sweet potatoes you'll ever eat. The recipe is easy to prepare and can be made ahead of time, making it a super-convenient addition to your family table.

## Serves: 6–8 people

3 lbs (1.4kg) sweet potatoes
8 tablespoons unsalted butter
½ cup white granulated sugar
½ cup light brown sugar
1 teaspoon ground cinnamon
½ teaspoon ground nutmeg
1 tablespoon pure vanilla extract
2 tablespoons maple syrup
1 teaspoon ginger paste

1. Preheat the oven to 375°F (190°C).

2. Clean and peel the sweet potatoes. Cut them into even 1-inch (2.5cm) slices. Place them in a 9 × 13-inch (23 × 33cm) baking dish and set aside.

3. In a nonstick medium skillet over a low heat, add the butter. Once fully melted, whisk in the granulated sugar and brown sugar until fully dissolved.

4. Whisk in the cinnamon, nutmeg, and vanilla extract until fully combined.

5. Whisk in the maple syrup and ginger paste until fully combined.

6. Pour this mixture over the sweet potatoes. Tightly cover the dish with aluminum foil.

7. Place the dish in the oven and bake for 1 hour (or longer if you like your sweet potatoes extra soft).

8. After an hour, remove the aluminum foil from the baking dish and allow the sweet potatoes to cook for an additional 15 minutes (or longer if you like your sweet potatoes extra soft) so the sauce can reduce.

9. Remove the dish from the oven and serve immediately.

# SWEET POTATO PIE

**PREP TIME: 20 MINUTES • COOK TIME: 45–60 MINUTES**

This classic Southern sweet potato pie is the perfect dessert to satisfy your sweet tooth. It's made with a puree of soft and creamy sweet potatoes and mixed with the perfect amount of sugar and spices like nutmeg, cinnamon, and vanilla extract. Then it's poured into a premade pie crust, but feel free to make it from scratch and bake it to perfection. It is guaranteed to not only fill your home with comfort but love as well. Serve it warm or cold and enjoy the comforting flavor of this classic Southern holiday treat.

## Serves: 8

9-inch (23cm) unbaked pie crust, store-bought or homemade

2 lbs (907g) sweet potatoes

½ cup unsalted butter, softened

1 cup granulated sugar

½ cup whole milk

2 large eggs

½ teaspoon ground nutmeg

1 teaspoon ground cinnamon

2 teaspoons pure vanilla extract

1. Preheat the oven to 350°F (180°C). Place the pie crust in a 9-inch (23cm) pie dish.

2. To a large pot, place the sweet potatoes and cover with water. Over high heat, bring to a boil and cook until softened.

3. Remove the pot from the heat, drain the water, and allow the sweet potatoes to cool.

4. In a large bowl, combine the sweet potatoes, butter, sugar, milk, eggs, nutmeg, cinnamon, and vanilla extract. Mix until fully combined (see tip). Pour the filling into the crust.

5. Place the pan in the oven and bake for 45–60 minutes or until a toothpick inserted into the center comes out clean.

6. Remove the pan from the oven and allow the pie to cool for 30 minutes before serving.

**TIP:** If you're using a stand mixer, place the softened sweet potatoes, butter, sugar, milk, eggs, nutmeg, cinnamon, and vanilla extract in the mixing bowl. Attach the paddle attachment to the stand mixer and mix on low speed until the ingredients are well combined and the mixture reaches a smooth consistency. Avoid overmixing, as it can lead to a dense or gummy texture in the final dish. If necessary, use a spatula to scrape down the sides of the bowl to ensure all the ingredients are evenly mixed.

# POOR MAN'S PEACH COBBLER

**PREP TIME: 20 MINUTES • COOK TIME: 40 MINUTES**

Everyone needs something sweet after dinner! Indulge yourself with this cobbler that's bursting with decadent flavors, such as fresh peaches, brown sugar, vanilla extract, nutmeg, cinnamon, and lemon. The combination of this blend and a luscious and sweet batter is sure to make an unforgettable dessert loved by all. Serve this warm with a dollop of whipped cream or a scoop of ice cream to elevate the experience!

## Serves: 8–10 people

6 yellow peaches (1½ lbs [680g]), peeled and cut into thick slices

1½ cups all-purpose flour

1 teaspoon kosher salt

1 teaspoon baking soda

1½ cups granulated sugar, divided

1 cup cold whole milk

½ cup light brown sugar

1 teaspoon pure vanilla extract

1 teaspoon ground cinnamon

1 teaspoon ground nutmeg

1 tablespoons freshly squeezed lemon juice

8 tablespoons unsalted butter

1. Preheat the oven to 350°F (180°C).

2. In a medium bowl, combine the flour, salt, baking soda, and 1 cup of granulated sugar. Slowly add the cold milk while whisking until it turns into a smooth batter.

3. In a large skillet over medium heat, combine 1 cup of water, the brown sugar, vanilla extract, cinnamon, nutmeg, lemon juice, and the remaining ½ cup of granulated sugar. Stir until the sugars are dissolved.

4. Add the peaches, reduce the heat to low, and bring to a simmer for 6–10 minutes depending on your texture preference.

5. Place the butter in a 9 × 13-inch (23 × 33cm) baking dish and place the dish in the oven.

6. Once the butter is melted, remove the dish from the oven and pour it into the batter. Add the peaches over the top, ensuring **NOT** to mix anything.

7. Return the dish to the oven and bake for 40 minutes.

8. Remove the dish from the oven and allow the cobbler to cool for 25 minutes before serving.

# SOUTHERN COMFORT

# SHRIMP PO' BOY

**PREP TIME: 15 MINUTES • COOK TIME: 15 MINUTES**

Never in a million years did I think the simple combination of fried shrimp, lettuce, tomato, and dill pickles packed into a delicious loaf of French bread would light up my taste buds this way. The shrimp po' boy is the perfect casual Southern comfort lunch, packed with flavor and certified to be a favorite among family and friends. Try this amazing recipe for an authentic taste of New Orleans cuisine right at home.

## Serves: 4

1 cup all-purpose flour

1 teaspoon Cajun seasoning

1 teaspoon smoked paprika

½ teaspoon garlic powder

½ teaspoon onion powder

1 teaspoon kosher salt

½ teaspoon freshly ground black pepper

¼ teaspoon ground cayenne (optional)

½ teaspoon dried thyme

Vegetable oil, for frying

1lb (454g) large shrimp, peeled and deveined

2 French bread leaves

¼ cup mayonnaise

1 cup shredded iceberg lettuce

Sliced tomatoes

Sliced dill pickles

1. In a large bowl, combine the flour, Cajun seasoning, smoked paprika, garlic powder, onion powder, salt, pepper, cayenne, and thyme. Mix well with a fork.

2. In a large skillet over medium heat, add 1 inch (2.5cm) of vegetable oil and heat until it reaches 350°F (180°C).

3. Coat the shrimp in the seasoned flour, shaking off any excess, then fry for 2 minutes on each side or until golden brown. Transfer the shrimp to a plate lined with paper towels to soak up the excess oil.

4. Cut the French bread loaves in half lengthwise and spread the mayonnaise on each half.

5. On the bottom halves, evenly distribute the lettuce, tomatoes, pickles, and fried shrimp. Top with the other halves of the bread. Cut the two loaves in half to make 4 servings.

6. Serve with a side of Homemade Remoulade Sauce (see page 198).

# SHRIMP & CHEESY SAVORY GRITS

**PREP TIME: 10 MINUTES • COOK TIME: 45 MINUTES**

Shrimp and grits, a true Southern comfort classic, can easily make you the most popular friend around with this recipe in your repertoire. The velvety grits are lovingly prepared in chicken broth, then elevated with the richness of butter, heavy cream, and a generous amount of shredded cheese. After all, who can resist a bowl of grits with a touch of indulgence?

## Serves: 2-4

4 cups chicken stock

1 teaspoon chicken bouillon

1 cup instant grits

4 tablespoons unsalted butter

¾ cup heavy cream, divided

½ cup shredded cheddar

4 strips thick-cut bacon

20 jumbo shrimp, 5lbs (2.3kg) total, deveined, tails on

1 teaspoon chili powder

1 teaspoon Old Bay seasoning

2 teaspoons garlic powder, divided

2 teaspoons seasoned salt, divided

2 teaspoons freshly ground black pepper, divided

½ cup diced sweet onion

½ cup diced green bell pepper

1 tablespoon minced garlic

½ cup grated Parmesan

1 teaspoon onion powder

1 teaspoon smoked paprika

2 medium lobster tails, removed from the shell, cleaned, deveined, and chopped (see tip)

2 tablespoons chopped green onions, for garnish

**Tip:** To remove lobster meat from the shell, use kitchen scissors to carefully cut along the soft underside of the tail. Lift the meat gently, keeping it attached at the narrow end, and then place it on top of the shell.

1. In a medium pot over high heat, combine the chicken stock and chicken bouillon. Bring to a boil.

2. Add the grits and stir continuously to avoid clumping.

3. Once the grits are a thick consistency, add the butter, ½ cup of the heavy cream, and the cheddar cheese. Reduce the heat to the lowest setting and stir periodically.

4. To a large skillet over medium-high heat, fry the bacon until it reaches your desired level of crunch. Transfer the bacon to a plate lined with paper towels. Leave the bacon fat in the skillet.

5. In a large bowl, combine the shrimp, chili powder, Old Bay seasoning, 1 teaspoon of garlic powder, 1 teaspoon of seasoned salt, and 1 teaspoon of black pepper. Toss well to coat.

6. Add the shrimp to the skillet over medium-high and sear for 2 minutes on each side.

Transfer the shrimp to a plate lined with paper towels. Leave the grease in the skillet.

7. Add the onion, bell pepper, and garlic. Sauté until soft.

8. Add the remaining ¼ cup heavy cream. Once it starts to bubble, reduce the heat to a medium-low and add the Parmesan. Stir until well combined.

9. Add the onion powder, smoked paprika, the remaining 1 teaspoon of garlic powder, the remaining 1 teaspoon of seasoned salt, and the remaining 1 teaspoon of black pepper. Mix until well combined.

10. Add the lobster tails and cook for 6 minutes or until the lobster is fully cooked.

11. Transfer everything in the skillet to a serving platter with the shrimp. Crumble the cooked bacon and sprinkle over the top. Garnish with the green onions. Serve over the grits and enjoy!

# CATFISH & GRITS
## WITH GARDEN CREAM SAUCE

**PREP TIME: 15 MINUTES • COOK TIME: 30 MINUTES**

Experience the amazing flavors of the South with this irresistible catfish and grits recipe. This dish brings together an amazing blend of flavors and textures that will leave you wanting more. The grits are slowly cooked with chicken broth, then enhanced with heavy cream, butter, gouda and Cheddar cheeses, and jalapeños for a kick. This results in delicious and creamy grits. The catfish fillets are coated in a homemade spice blend and fried to golden perfection before being served hot with the grits.

**Serves: 4**

3 cups chicken broth

1 tablespoon chicken bouillon

1 cup stone-ground grits

1½ cups heavy cream, divided

4 tablespoons unsalted butter, divided

¼ cup grated Gouda cheese

¼ cup grated cheddar cheese

2 tablespoons diced jalapeños

1 tablespoon all-purpose flour

1 cup cornmeal

½ tablespoon lemon pepper

1 teaspoon garlic powder

1 teaspoon ground oregano

1 teaspoon onion powder

1 teaspoon smoked paprika

2 teaspoons Old Bay Seasoning

2 teaspoons Cajun seasoning

4 catfish fillets, about 1-1½lbs (454-680g) total

1 tablespoon mustard

Vegetable oil, for frying

1 shallot, diced

½ green bell pepper, diced

½ red bell pepper, diced

2 tablespoons minced garlic

3 tablespoons tomato paste

¼ cup grated Parmesan

1. To a medium saucepan over high heat, add the chicken broth and bring to a boil. Add the chicken bouillon. Reduce the heat to low and slowly stir in the grits. Simmer for 20 minutes, stirring occasionally to avoid clumping.

2. Once the grits are thick and creamy (not grainy), add ½ cup of heavy cream, 2 tablespoons of butter, Gouda, cheddar, and jalapeño.

3. In a large shallow bowl, combine the flour, cornmeal, lemon pepper, garlic powder, oregano, onion powder, smoked paprika, and Old Bay seasoning.

4. Lightly season the catfish fillets with the Cajun seasoning, then apply a thin coat of mustard as a binder. Evenly coat the catfish in the cornmeal mixture.

5. To a large skillet or saucepan over medium heat, add 1 inch (2.5cm) of vegetable oil. Heat until the oil reaches 325°F (165°C). Add the catfish fillets and fry for 8 minutes or until golden brown.

6. Transfer the catfish to an elevated wire rack to drain the excess oil.

7. To a medium saucepan over medium heat, add the remaining 2 tablespoons of butter. Once the butter has melted, add the shallot, bell peppers, and garlic. Sauté until fragrant.

8. Stir in the tomato paste and cook for 1 minute.

9. Whisk in the remaining 1 cup of heavy cream until smooth. Add the Parmesan cheese and stir until melted. Remove the skillet from the heat.

10. To serve, plate the grits followed by the catfish fillets, and finish with the sauce on top.

# RED BEANS & RICE

**PREP TIME: 30 MINUTES (PLUS SOAKING TIME) • COOK TIME: 2–3 HOURS**

This is a classic Southern comfort dish I've never been able to get enough of. And adding a smoked turkey leg to it gives this recipe a rich and smoky flavor, while the andouille sausage adds the perfect amount of heat. The red beans are soaked overnight, leaving them tender and creamy when cooked, and are complemented by a flavorful blend of Cajun spices and aromatics. Serve these beans on a bed of fluffy white rice and top it with chopped green onions for the most satisfying home-cooked meal you'll ever eat.

## Serves: 6–8

1lb (454g) dry red beans

1 tablespoon canola oil

1 andouille sausage, sliced

1 green bell pepper, diced

1 large white or yellow onion, diced

2 celery stalks, diced

5 garlic cloves, minced

1 teaspoon Cajun seasoning

½ teaspoon smoked paprika

½ teaspoon ground cayenne

½ teaspoon freshly ground black pepper

4 cups chicken broth

2 tablespoons roasted chicken base

2 dried bay leaves

Smoked turkey leg, about 1-2lbs (454-907kg)

Kosher salt, to taste

Cooked white rice, for serving

Handful of chopped green onions, for serving

1. In a large bowl, cover the red beans in water and soak for 8 hours or overnight. Pick out any bad beans or debris.

2. Once the beans are soft, discard the water. Set aside the beans.

3. In a large pot or Dutch oven over medium heat, add the canola oil. Once the oil is hot, add the sausage and cook until charred and smoky on both sides. Transfer the sausage to a bowl and set aside.

4. Add the bell pepper, onion, celery, and garlic. Sauté until fragrant and soft.

5. Stir in the Cajun seasoning, smoked paprika, cayenne, and black pepper.

6. Add the sausage and chicken broth. Bring to a boil.

7. Once at a boil, add the roasted chicken base, red beans, bay leaves, and turkey leg. Reduce the heat to low and simmer for 2 hours.

8. Remove the turkey leg from the pot and allow to cool. Shred the meat and discard the skin and bones.

9. Stir the shredded meat into the pot and cook for 30 minutes more. Taste and add salt if needed.

10. Serve with white rice and chopped green onions.

# CHICKEN, SHRIMP & SAUSAGE GUMBO

**PREP TIME: 20 MINUTES • COOK TIME: 1 HOUR 40 MINUTES**

I love Cajun cuisine, especially a good, warm pot of gumbo. It was the first Cajun dish I ever learned how to make—and it's perfect for a cozy night in. The combination of andouille sausage, shrimp, and chicken cooked down in a rich broth creates a flavor palette that most have never experienced. While you'll need some strong wrists to stir that roux, the end product will be well worth it. Serve with green onions over a bed of white rice for a true Southern comfort experience.

## Serves: 6–8

½ cup canola oil

½ cup unsalted butter

1 cup all-purpose flour

1 white or yellow onion, diced

1 green bell pepper, diced

3 celery stalks, diced

5 garlic cloves, minced

2 teaspoons garlic powder

1 teaspoon onion powder

2 teaspoons smoked paprika

2 teaspoon Cajun seasoning

4 cups chicken broth

5 sprigs of thyme

2 dried bay leaves

½ teaspoon Old Bay seasoning

10oz (285g) cooked rotisserie chicken breast, cubed or shredded

1lb (454g) andouille sausage, sliced

1 tablespoon roasted chicken base

1lb (454g) large shrimp, peeled and deveined, tails on

1½ chopped green onions, green parts only

kosher salt, to taste (optional)

Cooked white rice, for serving

1. In a large pot or Dutch oven over low heat, add the oil and butter. Once the butter melts, increase the heat to medium, add the flour and whisk constantly for 30 minutes until the roux turns a dark chocolate color.

2. Add the onion, bell pepper, celery, and garlic. Sauté in the roux until the vegetables are tender and fragrant, about 5-8 minutes.

3. Stir in the garlic powder, onion powder, smoked paprika, and Cajun seasoning. Mix until well combined.

4. Slowly add in the chicken broth while whisking to break down any lumps. Bring to a boil, then add the thyme and bay leaves.

5. Stir in the Old Bay seasoning, cooked chicken, sausage, and roasted chicken base. Cook for 1 hour.

6. Add the shrimp, then remove and discard the bay leaves and thyme stems. Cook until the shrimp turn bright pink, about 6 minutes.

7. Stir in the green onions and taste for seasonings. Add salt if needed.

8. Serve with white rice and enjoy!

# ONE-POT SAUSAGE JAMBALAYA

**PREP TIME: 15 MINUTES • COOK TIME: 30 MINUTES**

Sausage jambalaya is a delicious one-pot meal that's perfect for a quick and filling family dinner. It's the most awesome combination of Cajun andouille sausage and tender sautéed vegetables, with a spicy kick from Cajun seasoning. Make sure to add fresh chopped green onions to bring this dish to its fullest potential. And don't forget to make room in your fridge because you'll have some delicious leftovers for a couple days!

## Serves: 6

2 tablespoons avocado oil

1lb (454g) andouille sausage, sliced

1 large white or yellow onion, diced

1 green bell pepper, diced

3 celery stalks, diced

5 garlic cloves, minced

1 teaspoon chili powder

1 teaspoon Cajun seasoning

1 teaspoon kosher salt

1 teaspoon smoked paprika

1 teaspoon garlic powder

1 teaspoon onion powder

1 teaspoon dried thyme

2 cups jasmine rice, rinsed (see tip)

2 medium tomatoes, diced

3 cups chicken stock

¾ cup chopped green onion, green parts only

1. To a large pot or Dutch oven over medium heat, add the avocado oil. Once the oil is hot, add the sausage and cook for 2 minutes per side or until slightly charred on both sides. Remove the sausage from the pot and set aside.

2. Add the onion, bell pepper, celery, and garlic to the pot and sauté for 3 minutes or until fragrant and soft.

3. Add the chili powder, Cajun seasoning, salt, smoked paprika, garlic powder, onion powder, and thyme. Stir until well combined.

4. Add the jasmine rice and stir until the rice takes on the color from the spices.

5. Add the diced tomatoes and chicken stock along with the sausage. Bring to a boil, then reduce the heat to low and simmer for 20 minutes.

6. Add the green onion and fluff the rice with a fork before serving.

**TIP:** To wash the rice, add it to a colander and rinse it under cold water until the water runs clear.

# SMOTHERED PORK CHOPS

**PREP TIME: 15 MINUTES • COOK TIME: 45 MINUTES**

Smothered pork chops are such an easy and comforting recipe. The bone-in chops are seasoned to perfection with a blend of simple spices, then dredged in seasoned flour before being fried until golden brown and crispy. Then they're smothered in a hearty homestyle onion and mushroom gravy. Serve them with rice or mashed potatoes and some veggies for a satisfying dish that will please the whole family.

## Serves: 4

### FOR THE PORK CHOPS

4 bone-in pork chops, about 4lbs (1.8kg) total

1 teaspoon garlic powder

2 teaspoons kosher salt

1 teaspoon freshly ground black pepper

1 teaspoon paprika

2 cups all-purpose flour

½ tablespoon Cajun seasoning

Vegetable oil, for frying

### FOR THE GRAVY

4 tablespoons unsalted butter

1 large white or yellow onion, chopped

5 garlic cloves, minced

1 cup sliced white mushrooms

4 tablespoons all-purpose flour

3 cups chicken broth

1 tablespoon roasted chicken base

2 teaspoons crushed red pepper flakes (optional)

2 teaspoons Cajun seasoning

2 teaspoons chopped fresh parsley

Kosher salt and freshly ground black pepper, to taste

1. To a large bowl, add the pork chops, garlic powder, salt, black pepper, and paprika. Massage the seasonings into the meat.

2. To a bowl or raised rim plate, add the flour and Cajun seasoning. Use a fork to mix until well combined.

3. Dredge the pork chops in the seasoned flour, shaking off any excess. Set aside.

4. To a large skillet over medium heat add 3 inches (7.5cm) of vegetable oil. Heat the oil to 350°F (180°C).

5. Once the oil is hot, add the pork chops and fry for 4–5 minutes on each side.

6. Remove the pork chops from the skillet and place them on an elevated wire rack to drain the excess oil.

7. To a separate large skillet over medium heat, add the butter. Once the butter has melted, add the onion, garlic, and mushrooms. Sauté until fragrant and tender, about 5 minutes.

8. Add the flour and stir until it dissolves. Slowly add the chicken broth while whisking to break up clumps. Add the roasted chicken base, red pepper flakes (if using), Cajun seasoning, parsley, and salt and pepper to taste.

9. Once the gravy starts to thicken, add the pork chops, basting them with the gravy. Simmer for 5–10 minutes or until the pork chops reach an internal temperature of 145°F (63°C).

10. Remove the skillet from the heat and allow the pork chops to rest for 5–10 minutes.

11. Serve with white rice or creamy mashed potatoes.

**VEGAN COMFORT**

# VEGAN MAC & CHEESE

**PREP TIME: 15 MINUTES • COOK TIME: 35 MINUTES**

Serve this vegan mac and cheese recipe at your next family gathering and see if anyone can guess that it's vegan! This dish is perfect for anyone looking for a dairy-free alternative to the classic comfort food of Southern baked mac and cheese. The cheese sauce is made with vegan cheddar, mozzarella, and Parmesan cheeses, along with a delicious blend of spices. It's very easy to make and packed with flavor, so give it a try and share with your favorite vegan friend!

## Serves: 4–6

- 1lb (454g) vegan elbow macaroni, cooked according to package instructions
- 4 tablespoons vegan butter
- 4 tablespoons all-purpose flour
- 3 cups unsweetened almond milk
- 1 cup shredded vegan cheddar cheese, divided
- 1 cup shredded vegan mozzarella, divided
- 2 tablespoons grated vegan Parmesan cheese
- 2 tablespoons Dijon mustard
- 1 teaspoon garlic powder
- 1 teaspoon smoked paprika, plus more
- 1 teaspoon onion powder
- 1 teaspoon kosher salt
- ½ teaspoon freshly ground black pepper
- ¼ cup breadcrumbs

1. Preheat the oven to 350°F (180°C).

2. Run the cooked macaroni under cold water and drain. Set aside.

3. To a large skillet over medium heat, add the butter. Once the butter has melted, whisk in the flour until combined.

4. Gradually add the almond milk while continuing to whisk to break down any lumps. Cook for 5 minutes or until the sauce thickens.

5. Reduce the heat to low and add ½ cup of vegan cheddar, ½ cup of the vegan mozzarella, the vegan Parmesan, Dijon mustard, garlic powder, smoked paprika, onion powder, the salt, and black pepper. Stir until the mixture is combined and creamy.

6. Add the cooked macaroni and stir until the pasta is fully covered with cheese sauce.

7. Transfer everything to a 9 × 13-inch (23 × 33cm) baking dish. Sprinkle the breadcrumbs, the remaining ½ cup of vegan cheddar, and the remaining ½ cup of mozzarella over the top. Sprinkle a little smoked paprika over the top for color.

8. Place the dish in the oven and bake for 20 minutes or until the breadcrumbs are golden brown and the cheeses have melted.

9. Serve hot and enjoy!

# VEGAN BAKED ZITI

**PREP TIME: 25 MINUTES • COOK TIME: 35 MINUTES**

Vegan baked ziti gives the classic Italian dish a run for its money with a vegetarian spin. Made with marinara sauce, tender ziti, and classic Italian herbs, then slowly baked together with vegan cheese, this dish is a plant-based-eater's dream. And I've made it even more tasty by adding plant-based beef. Get to cooking and enjoy all the flavors of a classic baked ziti knowing it's 100% cruelty-free.

## Serves: 6–8

2 tablespoons olive oil

1 yellow onion, diced

5 garlic cloves, minced

1lb (454g) vegan beef

2 tablespoons tomato paste

1 (24oz [680g]) can of marinara sauce

1 (15oz [425g]) can of crushed tomatoes

4 basil leaves, ripped

2 teaspoons ground oregano

2 teaspoons garlic powder

1 teaspoon onion powder

1 teaspoon red pepper flakes

Kosher salt and freshly ground black pepper, to taste

1lb (454g) vegan ziti, cooked according to package instructions

1 cup shredded vegan mozzarella

½ cup grated vegan Parmesan cheese

1. Preheat the oven to 375°F (190°C).

2. To a large skillet over medium heat, add the olive oil. Once the oil is hot, add the onion and garlic. Sauté for 5 minutes or until soft and fragrant.

3. Add the vegan beef to the skillet and brown for 6 minutes. Stir in the tomato paste and sauté for 1 minute.

4. Add the marinara sauce, crushed tomatoes, basil, oregano, garlic powder, onion powder, red pepper flakes, and salt and black pepper to taste. Stir to combine, then simmer for 15 minutes, stirring occasionally to prevent burning.

5. Add the cooked ziti to the sauce. Layer a 9 × 13-inch (23 × 33cm) baking dish with ziti first, then mozzarella and Parmesan. Repeat this step until you fill the baking dish, layering it with mozzarella as the final step. Cover the dish with aluminum foil.

6. Place the dish in the oven and bake for 20 minutes. Remove the foil and bake for 15 minutes more to allow the cheeses to melt and crisp slightly.

7. Remove the dish from the oven and allow the baked ziti to rest for 15 minutes before serving.

# VEGAN JERK JACKFRUIT TACOS

**PREP TIME: 15 MINUTES • COOK TIME: 30 MINUTES**

Vegan jackfruit "pulled pork" is a delicious meat-free alternative to actual pulled pork. The combination of the wood-smoked flavor from liquid smoke, barbecue sauce, and an array of spices turns the jackfruit into a pot bursting with flavor that's so good, you won't even be able to tell it's not meat. Assemble with fresh cilantro and avocado for a quick and nutritious weeknight dinner for your friends and family.

## Serves: 4–6

2 (8oz [227g]) cans of jackfruit, in brine

1 tablespoon avocado oil

½ white onion, diced

5 garlic cloves, minced

½ cup vegetable broth

¼ cup store-bought honey barbecue sauce

½ tablespoon soy sauce

½ tablespoon Worcestershire sauce

1 teaspoon liquid smoke

½ teaspoon smoked paprika

½ teaspoon ground cumin

½ teaspoon chili powder

1½ teaspoon jerk seasoning

Kosher salt and black pepper, to taste

10 corn tortillas

½ cup chopped fresh cilantro

½ cup diced red onion, soaked in water

1 avocado, diced

1. Drain and rinse the jackfruit. Pat dry with paper towels. Use a fork to shred the jackfruit into small pieces that look similar to shredded pork.

2. To a large skillet over medium heat, add the avocado oil. Once the oil is hot, add the onions and garlic. Sauté until fragrant and soft, about 5 minutes.

3. Add the jackfruit and cook, stirring occasionally for 5 minutes or until the jackfruit begins to brown.

4. Stir in the vegetable broth, honey barbecue sauce, soy sauce, Worcestershire sauce, and liquid smoke. Mix until well combined.

5. Stir in the smoked paprika, cumin, chili powder, jerk seasoning, and salt and black pepper to taste. Cook for 10 minutes or until the jackfruit is tender and the sauce has thickened.

6. Assemble your tacos with a spoonful of jackfruit in each tortilla. Add the cilantro, red onion, and avocado.

7. Serve and enjoy!

# VEGAN COCONUT & CURRY CHICKPEAS

**PREP TIME: 10 MINUTES • COOK TIME: 20 MINUTES**

This is a flavor-packed vegan delight that's also a healthy and tasty option for a simple family dinner. This dish is packed with protein and nutrients, giving you the perfect amount of healthfulness while still being savory. The coconut milk and curry base gives the chickpeas a creamy texture. Serve with rice or naan bread and garnish with cilantro for a filling meal that will satisfy the whole family.

## Serves: 4–6

1 tablespoon coconut oil

1 yellow onion, diced

5 garlic cloves, minced

1 tablespoon minced ginger

1 (14oz [425g]) can of crushed tomatoes

1 teaspoon dried thyme

¼ teaspoon ground allspice

1 tablespoon Jamaican curry powder

½ teaspoon ground cumin

½ teaspoon ground turmeric

¼ teaspoon garam masala

2 (14oz[425g]) cans of chickpeas, drained and rinsed

1 cup coconut milk

Kosher salt and freshly ground black pepper, to taste

½ cup chopped fresh cilantro

1. To a large skillet over medium heat, add the coconut oil. Once the oil is hot, add the onion, garlic, and ginger. Sauté for 3 minutes or until fragrant.

2. Add the crushed tomatoes and simmer for 3 minutes. Stir in the thyme, allspice, curry powder, cumin, turmeric, and garam masala. Mix until well combined.

3. Add the chickpeas and coconut milk. Stir until well combined. Simmer for 15 minutes or until the chickpeas are tender and the sauce thickens.

4. Add salt and pepper to taste.

5. Transfer everything in the skillet to a serving platter. Garnish with cilantro and serve with basmati rice.

# VEGAN KOREAN BARBECUE WINGS

**PREP TIME: 15 MINUTES · COOK TIME: 30 MINUTES**

Looking for a delicious alternative to traditional wings? These Korean barbecue fried cauliflower bites are just what you need to satisfy your cravings for something sweet, spicy, and crispy. These bites are perfect for sharing with friends or enjoying as a meat-free indulgence all to yourself.

## Serves: 4

### FOR THE BARBECUE SAUCE

¼ cup soy sauce

¼ cup light brown sugar

2 tablespoons sesame oil

2 tablespoons rice wine vinegar

2 garlic cloves, minced

½ tablespoon minced ginger

1 tablespoon gochujang

1½ tablespoons sesame seeds

### FOR THE WINGS

1 cup all-purpose flour

1 cup unsweetened almond milk

1 tablespoon garlic powder

1 tablespoon onion powder

1 teaspoon chili powder

1 teaspoon smoked paprika

½ teaspoon ground oregano

Kosher salt and freshly ground black pepper, to taste

2 lb (907g) head of cauliflower, cut into bite-sized pieces

Vegetable oil, for frying

Chopped green onions, to garnish

1. To make the wings, in a large bowl, combine the flour, almond milk, garlic powder, onion powder, chili powder, smoked paprika, oregano, and salt and pepper to taste. Mix until smooth.

2. Add the cauliflower and mix until fully coated in the batter.

3. Fill a large pot or Dutch oven halfway with vegetable oil set over medium heat. Once the oil reaches 350°F (177°C), working in small batches, add the cauliflower and fry for 5 minutes or until golden brown.

4. Transfer the cooked cauliflower to an elevated wire rack to drain the excess oil.

5. To make the barbecue sauce, heat a medium skillet over low heat. Add all the ingredients and whisk until well combined. Bring to a simmer and continue whisking until the sugar is fully dissolved.

6. Remove the skillet from the heat and allow the sauce to cool to room temperature.

7. In a large bowl, combine the barbecue sauce and fried cauliflower. Toss to fully coat.

8. Garnish with green onions and serve with vegan ranch or blue cheese dressing.

# FAMILY DINNER TIME

# ONE-POT CHICKEN & RICE

**PREP TIME: 15 MINUTES • COOK TIME: 30 MINUTES**

This Cajun-inspired one-pot chicken and rice dish is bursting with bold flavors and is super easy to make. The chicken thighs are seasoned with a blend of spices and seared to perfection, then combined with sautéed aromatic vegetables and jasmine rice slowly cooked down in chicken stock in the same pan. This dish is perfect for a quick weeknight dinner and is sure to be a favorite at the family table.

## Serves: 3–4

- 5 bone-in chicken thighs with skin, about 1½ lbs (680kg) total
- 1½ tablespoons Cajun seasoning, divided
- 2 teaspoons garlic powder
- 2 teaspoons ground cayenne
- 4 teaspoons ground turmeric, divided
- 2 teaspoons freshly ground black pepper
- 2 tablespoons avocado oil
- ½ cup diced red bell pepper
- ½ cup white onion, diced
- 1 tablespoon minced garlic
- 1 teaspoon chicken bouillon
- 2 cups jasmine rice, washed (see tip)
- 4 cups chicken stock

1. In a large bowl, combine the chicken thighs, 1 tablespoon of Cajun seasoning, garlic powder, cayenne, 2 teaspoons of turmeric, and black pepper. Massage the seasonings into the meat.

2. To a large, deep skillet or pan over medium heat, add the avocado oil. Once the oil is hot, add the chicken skin side down and sear for 6 minutes on each side. Remove the chicken from the pan and set aside.

3. To the same large pan, add the red bell pepper, onion, and garlic. Sauté until fragrant, about 5 minutes.

4. Add the chicken bouillon, the remaining 1½ teaspoons of Cajun seasoning, and the remaining 2 teaspoons of turmeric. Mix well until combined.

5. Add the jasmine rice and stir until it takes the colors from the seasoning and soaks up all the oil.

6. Add the chicken stock and return the chicken to the pan. Reduce the heat to medium-low, cover the pan, and steam for 20–25 minutes.

7. Serve and enjoy!

**TIP:** To wash the rice, add it to a colander and rinse it under cold water until the water runs clear.

# CHICKEN & BROCCOLI ALFREDO

**PREP TIME: 15 MINUTES • COOK TIME: 25 MINUTES**

This recipe is one of the easiest and most basic pasta dishes known to humankind. Enjoy it for a weeknight dinner or surprise a special someone with a fine dining experience. The creamy alfredo sauce pairs perfectly with the juicy chicken and tender broccoli, creating a flavorful and satisfying meal. With simple and straightforward ingredients—and minimal instructions—this recipe is sure to become a favorite for anyone looking for something quick and tasty to whip up!

## Serves: 4

1lb (454g) fettuccine

2 (8oz [227g]) boneless, skinless chicken breasts, butterflied and tenderized

2 teaspoons chicken bouillon, divided

1¼ teaspoon smoked paprika, divided

2 teaspoons garlic powder, divided

2 teaspoons onion powder, divided

1 teaspoon freshly ground black pepper, divided

2 tablespoons avocado oil

2 cups broccoli florets

4 tablespoons unsalted butter

1 shallot, finely diced

5 garlic cloves, minced

½ tablespoon minced fresh thyme

1 teaspoon crushed red pepper flakes (optional)

¼ teaspoon ground oregano

1½ cups heavy cream

1 cup grated Parmesan

Parsley, to garnish

1. Cook the fettuccine according to the package instructions. Reserve 2–3 tablespoons of pasta water and set the pasta aside.

2. In a large bowl, combine the chicken breasts with 1 teaspoon of chicken bouillon, ¼ teaspoon of smoked paprika, 1 teaspoon of garlic powder, 1 teaspoon of onion powder, and ½ teaspoon of black pepper. Massage the seasonings into the chicken.

3. To a large cast-iron skillet over medium-high heat, add the avocado oil. Once the oil is hot, add the chicken and sear on both sides for 6 minutes or until cooked through. You can use an instant-read thermometer to check the doneness—it should be at least 165°F.

4. To a small saucepan over medium heat, add 1 inch (2.5cm) of water and the broccoli. Cover and steam until the broccoli becomes tender.

5. To a large nonstick skillet over medium heat, add the butter. Once melted, add the shallot, garlic, and thyme. Sauté for 1 minute or until tender and fragrant.

6. Add the red pepper flakes (if using), the oregano, the remaining 1 teaspoon of chicken bouillon, the remaining 1 teaspoon of smoked paprika, the remaining 1 teaspoon of garlic powder, the remaining 1 teaspoon of onion powder, and the remaining black pepper. Stir until fragrant.

7. Slowly add the cream while whisking continuously. Bring to a simmer, then reduce the heat to low and add the Parmesan. Cook until the cheese sauce becomes thick, about 2–3 minutes.

8. Add the cooked fettuccine, reserved pasta water, and broccoli florets. Stir until the pasta is coated in the sauce, then serve immediately with sliced chicken breasts and garnish with the parsley.

# BUFFALO CHICKEN MAC & CHEESE

**PREP TIME: 15 MINUTES • COOK TIME: 35–40 MINUTES**

This buffalo chicken mac and cheese takes a classic staple to new heights. It's loaded with flavorful shredded chicken, buffalo sauce, and a cheese blend that's bound to satisfy any cheese lover's cravings. Impress your friends and family with this elevated recipe and soon-to-be party favorite!

## Serves: 6–8

2 (8oz [227g]) boneless, skinless chicken breasts

1 teaspoon poultry seasoning

2 teaspoons onion powder, divided

2 teaspoons garlic powder, divided

1 teaspoon chicken bouillon

2 tablespoons avocado oil

1 cup buffalo sauce, divided

4 tablespoons unsalted butter

4 tablespoons all-purpose flour

3 cups heavy whipping cream

8 ounces (227g) shredded fontina cheese, divided

8 ounces (227g) shredded sharp cheddar cheese, divided

1 teaspoon kosher salt

1 teaspoon freshly ground black pepper

½ teaspoon chili powder

¼ cup crumbled blue cheese

3 cups elbow macaroni, cooked a couple minutes shy of package instructions

1. Preheat the oven to 350°F (180°C). Grease a 9 × 13-inch (23 × 33cm) baking dish and set aside.

2. In a large bowl, combine the chicken breasts, poultry seasoning, 1 teaspoon of onion powder, 1 teaspoon of garlic powder, and chicken bouillon.

3. To a large skillet over medium heat, add the avocado oil. Once the oil is hot, add the chicken breasts and sear on both sides for 6 minutes each. Once the chicken is fully cooked, use a fork to shred the meat.

4. Transfer the shredded chicken to a large bowl. Add ½ cup of buffalo sauce and mix until well combined. Set aside.

5. To a large skillet over low heat, add the butter. Once the butter is melted, add the flour and whisk until combined to create a roux.

6. Slowly add the cream while continuing to whisk. Bring the sauce to a simmer, then remove the skillet from the heat.

7. Add a ¼ pound (113g) of fontina, a ¼ pound (113g) of sharp cheddar, salt, pepper, chili powder, the remaining 1 teaspoon of garlic powder, the remaining 1 teaspoon of onion powder, and the remaining ½ cup of buffalo sauce. Mix until well combined.

8. Add the cooked macaroni and shredded buffalo chicken to the cheese sauce. Mix until well combined.

9. Transfer the macaroni and cheese to the prepared baking dish and top with the blue cheese, the remaining ¼ pound (113g) of fontina, and the remaining ¼ pound (113g) of sharp cheddar.

10. Place the dish in the oven and bake for 25–30 minutes.

11. Remove the dish from the oven and allow the mac and cheese to cool for a few minutes before serving.

# HOT HONEY CHICKEN SANDWICHES

**PREP TIME: 20 MINUTES (PLUS MARINATING TIME) • COOK TIME: 20–25 MINUTES**

Want to learn how to make the best fried chicken sandwiches at home? These hot honey fried chicken sandwiches are the truth. Juicy chicken thighs are marinated in a blend of spices and buttermilk, coated in seasoned flour, and fried to perfection. But what really takes this sandwich to the next level is the homemade hot honey sauce made from sriracha, buffalo sauce, and a drizzle of honey for the perfect blend of spicy and sweet.

## Serves: 6

6 boneless, skinless chicken thighs, about 2lbs (907kg) total, tenderized to even thickness (see tip)

4 teaspoons chicken bouillon, divided

2 teaspoons chili powder, divided

2 teaspoons smoked paprika, divided

2 teaspoons onion powder, divided

2 teaspoons garlic powder, divided

2 teaspoons kosher salt, divided

2 teaspoons freshly ground black pepper, divided

½ cup buttermilk

Vegetable oil, for frying

1 cup all-purpose flour

4 tablespoons unsalted butter

1 cup buffalo sauce, divided

¼ cup sriracha sauce

½ cup honey

6 brioche buns, lightly toasted

½ cup mayonnaise (optional)

1 cup shredded lettuce

1 tomato, sliced

12 dill pickle slices (optional)

1. In a large bowl, combine the chicken, 2 teaspoons of chicken base, 1 teaspoon of chili powder, 1 teaspoon of smoked paprika, 1 teaspoon of onion powder, 1 teaspoon of garlic powder, 1 teaspoon of salt, and 1 teaspoon of black pepper. Massage the seasonings into the meat.

2. Add the buttermilk, cover, and refrigerate to marinate for 2–24 hours.

3. To a large pot or Dutch oven over medium heat, add 4 inches (10cm) of vegetable oil and heat to 325°F (165°C).

4. In a large bowl, combine the flour, the remaining 2 teaspoons of chicken bouillon, the remaining 1 teaspoon of chili powder, the remaining 1 teaspoon of smoked paprika, the remaining 1 teaspoon of onion powder, the remaining 1 teaspoon of garlic powder, the remaining 1 teaspoon of salt, and the remaining 1 teaspoon of black pepper. Mix well.

5. One thigh at a time, dredge the marinated chicken in the seasoned flour and shake off any excess.

6. Working in batches, add the chicken to the pot and fry for 12–15 minutes.

7. To a large skillet over low heat, add the butter. Once melted, whisk in the buffalo sauce, sriracha, and honey. Simmer for 4–5 minutes. Allow the sauce to cool to room temperature before brushing it on the fried chicken thighs.

8. Assemble the sandwiches by adding mayo (if using) to the bottom bun, followed by chicken, lettuce, tomato, and dill pickles (if using). Top with the top bun and serve immediately.

**TIP:** You can use a meat mallet or a tenderizing tool to pound the chicken. Place the chicken thighs between two sheets of plastic wrap or wax paper to avoid making a mess and gently pound them until they are even.

# BOURBON CHICKEN

**PREP TIME: 15 MINUTES • COOK TIME: 30 MINUTES**

This recipe is just what you need when you're in the mood for something sweet and savory. It's got everything you want: juicy chicken seasoned with salt, pepper, and ground ginger for an extra kick—and it's cooked in a sticky homemade bourbon sauce made with real bourbon, hoisin sauce, brown sugar, honey, and fresh garlic and ginger. The flavor profile is so delicious that you'll be licking your fingers clean, especially when you serve it up with some steamed jasmine rice. Make sure to garnish with green onions.

## Serves: 4–6

8 boneless, skinless chicken thighs, cut into bite-sized pieces, about 2lbs (907kg) total

2 teaspoons kosher salt

2 teaspoons freshly ground black pepper

2 teaspoons onion powder

1 teaspoon ground ginger

3 tablespoons avocado oil

2 tablespoons cornstarch

½ cup low-sodium soy sauce

½ cup bourbon

¼ cup hoisin sauce

½ cup light brown sugar

2 tablespoons apple cider vinegar

1 tablespoon honey

3 garlic cloves, minced

2 tablespoons minced fresh ginger

Chopped green onions, to garnish

1. In a large bowl, combine the chicken thighs, salt, pepper, onion powder, and ginger. Massage the seasonings into the meat.

2. To a medium skillet over medium heat, add the avocado oil. Once the oil is hot, add the thighs and cook for 15–20 minutes or until fully cooked. Remove the chicken from the skillet and set aside.

3. In a small dish, combine the cornstarch and 2 tablespoons of water to create a slurry. Set aside.

4. To the same skillet, add the soy sauce and bourbon, and cook for 5 minutes to cook out the alcohol.

5. Add the hoisin sauce, brown sugar, apple cider vinegar, honey, garlic, and ginger. Bring to a simmer for 2–3 minutes before adding the cornstarch slurry to thicken the consistency.

6. Return the cooked chicken to the skillet and stir until the thighs are coated in the sauce. Cook for 5 minutes more.

7. Garnish with green onions and serve with jasmine rice.

# STUFFED PEPPERS

**PREP TIME: 15 MINUTES • COOK TIME: 45 MINUTES**

These stuffed bell peppers are filled with flavor from savory ground beef, yellow rice, and a variety of vegetables. Topping these peppers with melted pepper jack cheese gives this recipe an unforgettable finish. This is a perfect recipe for a hearty weeknight dinner!

## Serves: 6

6 bell peppers, any color

2 tablespoons avocado oil

1lb (454g) 80% lean ground beef

2 teaspoons adobo

1 teaspoon kosher salt

1 teaspoon freshly ground black pepper

1 teaspoon chili powder

1 teaspoon smoked paprika

1 white onion, diced

2 tablespoons minced garlic

1 cup corn kernels

1 cup black beans

1 cup tomato sauce

3 cups Yellow Rice (page 185)

2 cups shredded pepper jack cheese

1. Preheat the oven to 350 (180°C).

2. Cut the tops off the bell peppers. Remove the cores and clean out the inside and all the seeds using water. Don't let the tops of the bell peppers go to waste—finely dice them and use 1 cup for your filling. Place the peppers in a 9 × 13-inch (23 × 33cm) baking dish and set aside.

3. To a large nonstick skillet over medium heat, add the avocado oil. Once the oil is hot, add the ground beef and cook until browned.

4. Add the adobo, salt, pepper, chili powder, and smoked paprika. Stir the seasonings into the ground beef until evenly distributed.

5. Add the onion, garlic, corn, black beans, tomato sauce, yellow rice, and diced pepper tops. Mix until everything is evenly combined. Stuff the peppers with the mixture and generously top with pepper jack cheese.

6. Place the baking dish in the oven and bake the peppers for 30 minutes.

7. Serve and enjoy!

# CHUCK ROAST BEEF STEW

**PREP TIME: 15 MINUTES • COOK TIME: 3 HOURS**

Savor the comforting flavors of this delectable chuck roast beef stew. Succulent pieces of chuck roast are seasoned to perfection with an array of spices, then seared to lock in all the incredible flavors. The beef is gently simmered in a flavorful combination of beef broth, onions, garlic, carrots, thyme, rosemary, bay leaves, and celery, infusing your home with a tantalizing aroma. To add a delightful texture, Yukon Gold potatoes are included in the stew. Serve this piping hot stew alongside a bed of rice for a truly satisfying comfort meal that's sure to leave you fully satisfied.

## Serves: 4–6

2½lbs (1.1kg) chuck roast beef, cut into 1-inch (2.5cm) cubes

2 teaspoons kosher salt, plus more

1 teaspoon freshly ground black pepper, plus more

2 teaspoons onion powder

2 teaspoons garlic powder

2 tablespoons avocado oil

1 white onion, chopped

4 garlic cloves, minced

3 celery stalks, chopped

3 carrots, chopped

1 tablespoon tomato paste

1 tablespoon roasted beef base

¼ cup all-purpose flour

4 cups beef bone broth

3 dried bay leaves

6 sprigs of thyme

2 sprigs of rosemary

3 cups Yukon Gold potatoes

1½ cups frozen peas

1. In a large bowl, combine the beef, salt, pepper, onion powder, and garlic powder.

2. To a large pot or Dutch oven over medium heat, add the avocado oil. Once the oil is hot, sear the cubed beef on all sides until a brown crust forms, about 8 minutes total. Remove the beef from the pot and set aside.

3. To the same pot, add the onion, garlic, celery, and carrots. Sauté until soft, about 5 minutes.

4. Add the tomato paste and the roasted beef base and stir to coat the vegetables. Sprinkle in the flour and stir until it dissolves.

5. Return the beef to the pot and add the beef bone broth, bay leaves, thyme, rosemary, and salt and pepper to taste. Cover the pot and bring to a boil.

6. Once at a boil, reduce the heat to low and simmer for 2 hours.

7. Add the potatoes and peas. Cook for another 30–45 minutes or until the potatoes are tender.

8. Serve hot with rice and enjoy!

# CLASSIC POT ROAST

**PREP TIME: 30 MINUTES • COOK TIME: 3 HOURS 30 MINUTES**

Indulge in a comforting meal with the luxurious taste of beef slowly braised in red wine. This dish is a culinary masterpiece and a feel-good classic that will take your taste buds to a cozy and comforting space. The chuck is tender and juicy, seared to perfection to lock in all the flavor, and then slowly braised in a mixture of red wine, beef broth, and aromatic herbs such as thyme, garlic, and rosemary, creating an unforgettable smell that will warm your entire house up. The addition of carrots and tender celery adds a delightful contrast in texture and flavor to the beef. Pair the pot roast with a creamy bed of mashed potatoes and prepare for the ultimate food coma.

## Serves: 6–8

3 lb (1.4kg) chuck roast

½ tablespoon garlic powder

½ tablespoon onion powder

Kosher salt and freshly ground black pepper, to taste

2 tablespoons avocado oil

1 cup red wine

3 beef bouillon cubes

1 large onion, chopped

2 heads of garlic, cut in half

2 cups beef broth

1 tablespoon Worcestershire sauce

Handful of fresh parsley

10 sprigs of thyme

4 sprigs of rosemary

5 large carrots, peeled and cut into 2-inch (5cm) pieces

5 celery stalks, cut into 2-inch (5cm) pieces

1. Preheat the oven to 325°F (165°C).

2. Place the chuck roast on a baking sheet. Season with the garlic powder, onion powder, and salt and pepper to taste.

3. To a large Dutch oven over medium heat, add the avocado oil. Once the oil is hot, add the roast and sear on all sides until browned, about 8–10 minutes total. Remove the roast from the Dutch oven and set aside.

4. Deglaze the bottom of the pot with the red wine, then add the beef bouillon cubes and stir with a wooden spoon until they dissolve.

5. Add the onion and garlic, then place the roast on top of them. Add the beef broth, Worcestershire sauce, parsley, thyme, and rosemary. Bring the liquid to a simmer.

6. Place the covered Dutch oven in the oven and roast for 3 hours.

7. After 3 hours, taste the broth and adjust the seasonings to your liking.

8. Add the carrots and celery. Return the Dutch oven to the oven and roast for 30 minutes more.

9. Remove the Dutch oven from the oven and shred the cooked meat.

10. Serve the pot roast over mashed potatoes or rice and enjoy!

# GARLIC & HERB STEAK BITES

**PREP TIME: 15 MINUTES • COOK TIME: 15 MINUTES**

Everyone adores a quick-and-easy recipe, but what about one that's quick and gourmet? These steak bites will fulfill your desires. They're seasoned to perfection with a simple blend of salt, pepper, and garlic powder before being seared in a hot cast-iron skillet, allowing them to develop a mouthwatering crust. Sautéed shallots, rosemary, thyme, and garlic create a fragrant and flavorful sauce. Serve these exquisite steak bites immediately and relish each and every delectable bite.

## Serves: 4

2 (12oz [340g] each) New York strip steaks, cut into 1-inch (2.5cm) cubes

Kosher salt and freshly ground black pepper, to taste

1 teaspoon garlic powder

3 tablespoons grapeseed oil

4 tablespoons unsalted butter

½ shallot, diced

2 sprigs of rosemary

3 sprigs of thyme

2 tablespoons minced garlic

1 tablespoon finely chopped parsley, to garnish

1. In a large bowl, combine the steak cubes, salt, black pepper, and garlic powder.

2. To a large cast-iron skillet over medium heat, add the grapeseed oil. Once the oil is hot, add the steak cubes and sear on each side. Sear them hot and fast to develop a crust without overcooking. Remove the steak from the skillet and set aside.

3. Turn off the heat and allow the skillet to cool. Use paper towels to wipe out the excess oil.

4. Place the skillet over low heat and add the butter. Once the butter is melted, raise the heat to medium. Add the shallot and sauté until translucent.

5. Add the rosemary and thyme, and sauté until fragrant. Add the garlic last to prevent burning and sauté until fragrant.

6. Return the steak to the pan and toss the bites in the butter sauce. Transfer everything to a serving platter.

7. Top the steak bites with fresh parsley and toss one last time before serving.

# BIRRIA RAMEN

**PREP TIME: 30 MINUTES • COOK TIME: 5–6 HOURS**

We all grew to know and love birria tacos. Now take those deeply satisfying and aromatic flavors and turn them into ramen! The combination of dried chili peppers, herbs, and spices infuse the consommé with complex flavors. Tender pieces of chuck roast are then slow-cooked in the consommé until they soak up every bit of flavor. Serving this over ramen noodles makes a delicious meal that will warm you right up!

## Serves: 6–8

2 lb (907g) chuck roast, cut into 3-inch (7.5cm) cubes

1½ tablespoons kosher salt, divided

1 tablespoon freshly ground black pepper, divided

2 teaspoons adobo

3 tablespoons grapeseed oil

1 cup beef broth

5 dried guajillo chili peppers

2 dried ancho chili peppers

10 dried chiles de árbol

8 sprigs of thyme

2 bay leaves

8 garlic cloves

1 cinnamon stick

1 white or yellow onion, cut in half

6 whole allspice berries

1 tablespoon garlic powder

1 tablespoon chili powder

1 teaspoon ground cumin

2 3-ounce packs of ramen noodles

½ red onion, diced, for serving

1 tablespoon chopped fresh cilantro, for serving

1. In a large bowl, combine the chuck roast, ½ tablespoon of salt, ½ tablespoon of black pepper, and the adobo. Use your hands to ensure the meat is well seasoned.

2. To a Dutch oven over medium heat, add the grapeseed oil. Once the oil is hot, sear the chuck roast on all sides, about 8 minutes total. Remove the chuck roast from the Dutch oven and set aside.

3. Allow the Dutch oven to cool down, then use paper towels to wipe out any excess oil. Add the beef broth and use a wooden spoon to deglaze the bottom.

4. Return the beef to the Dutch oven over medium heat. Add 7 cups of water, the guajillo chili peppers, ancho chili peppers, chiles de árbol, thyme, bay leaves, garlic cloves, cinnamon stick, halved onion, and allspice berries. Bring to a boil, then reduce the heat to low and simmer for 1 hour.

5. Transfer the chili peppers, onion halves, thyme, and garlic cloves to a blender. Add the garlic powder, chili powder cumin, the remaining 1 tablespoon of salt, and the remaining ½ tablespoon of black pepper. Use a small amount of the broth from the Dutch oven to help blend smoother. Blend on high until the mixture forms a smooth red purée.

6. Pour the mixture into the Dutch oven and allow it to stew for 3–4 hours.

7. Once the beef is soft and tender, remove it from the consommé, and use two forks to shred it. Use the consommé (with the bay leaves removed) to boil store-bought ramen noodles until soft.

8. Plate the ramen with the beef, red onions, and cilantro. Serve and enjoy!

# LASAGNA ROLL UPS

**PREP TIME: 15 MINUTES • COOK TIME: 45 MINUTES**

These pasta rollups are a fun twist on a classic that's sure to be a family favorite at dinnertime! Everything we know and love about lasagna is rolled up into tender lasagna noodles. The flavorful meat sauce and creamy ricotta cheese create a delectable dish! This is a crowd-pleaser that can be served with garlic bread or your favorite green salad.

## Serves: 3–4

### FOR THE SAUCE

1 tablespoon olive oil

½ cup diced shallots

6 garlic cloves, minced

3 tablespoons tomato paste

1 (16oz [454g]) can of crushed tomatoes

2 teaspoons ground oregano

2 teaspoons garlic powder

Sea salt, to taste

2 teaspoons freshly ground black pepper

5 fresh basil leaves, sliced

### FOR THE ROLL UPS

1 tablespoon olive oil

1½ lbs (680g) ground beef

2 teaspoons seasoned salt

1 teaspoon crushed red pepper flakes

1 cup ricotta

¼ cup chopped fresh parsley

1 large egg

¼ cup Parmesan

6–8 lasagna noodles, cooked until al dente according to package instructions

2 cups shredded mozzarella

1. To make the tomato sauce, to a skillet over medium heat, add the olive oil. Once the oil is hot, add the shallots and garlic. Sauté until fragrant.

2. Stir in the tomato paste and crushed tomatoes. Add the oregano, garlic powder, salt to taste, and pepper. Mix until well combined.

3. Add the basil and cook the sauce over medium-low heat for 8 minutes. Remove the skillet from the heat and set aside.

4. To a large nonstick skillet over medium heat, add the olive oil. Once the oil is hot, add the beef and seasoned salt. Cook for 6–8 minutes or until the meat is browned.

5. Add the tomato sauce and red pepper flakes. Cook for 5 minutes more.

6. Preheat the oven to 350°F (180°C).

7. In a large bowl, combine the ricotta, parsley, egg, and Parmesan.

8. Place a lasagna noodle on a cutting board or another work surface. Spread the ricotta mixture about ½-inch (1cm) thick, followed by the meat sauce. Roll the lasagna up like you're making a cinnamon roll.

9. In a baking dish, spread half the remaining meat sauce on the bottom, evenly space the lasagna rolls, and coat them with the remaining meat sauce. Sprinkle the mozzarella over the top.

10. Place the dish in the oven and bake for 20–30 minutes.

11. Serve and enjoy!

# SPICY RIGATONI

**PREP TIME: 10 MINUTES • COOK TIME: 30 MINUTES**

This spicy rigatoni with Italian sausage and tomato cream sauce is the most delicious and satisfying meal, perfect for a weeknight dinner. The rigatoni is cooked to perfection and then tossed in a flavor-packed sauce made from scratch with Italian sausage, crushed tomatoes, fresh garlic, basil, and seasonings. The Parmesan cheese and heavy cream give it an unforgettable texture while also helping to balance out the spice. Feel free to adjust the spice or omit it completely based on your preference. Serve it with some breadsticks and a side salad for the full dining-out feeling that will please everyone at your table.

## Serves: 4–6

1lb (454g) rigatoni pasta

2 tablespoons avocado oil

½ teaspoon crushed red pepper flakes

4 garlic cloves, minced

1lb (454g) Italian sausage, casings removed

1 (28oz [794g]) can of crushed tomatoes

1 teaspoon garlic powder

1 teaspoon onion powder

¼ cup chopped fresh basil

Kosher salt and freshly ground black pepper, to taste

½ cup heavy cream

½ cup grated Parmesan

1. Cook the rigatoni according to the package instructions. Reserve ½ cup of pasta water, then drain the rest and set the pasta aside.

2. To a large skillet over medium heat, add the avocado oil. Once the oil is hot, add the red pepper flakes and garlic, and cook until fragrant.

3. Add the Italian sausage and brown it while breaking it up with a wooden spoon for 8 minutes or until fully cooked.

4. Stir in the crushed tomatoes, garlic powder, onion powder, basil, and salt and pepper, to taste. Simmer for 15 minutes.

5. Add the heavy cream and Parmesan and stir until well combined. If the sauce is too thick, gradually add the reserved pasta water until it reaches your desired thickness.

6. Add the cooked rigatoni to the sauce and stir to fully coat.

7. Serve and enjoy!

# INSTANT POT PULLED PORK SANDWICHES
## WITH HOMEMADE APPLE SLAW

**PREP TIME: 15–20 MINUTES • COOK TIME: 1 HOUR**

Get ready to rock your taste buds with one of my favorite sandwiches! You can enjoy everything you love about slow-cooked barbecue in under 1 hour. Simply coat thick pieces of pork shoulder with a homemade sweet rub then pressure-cook it in your favorite barbecue sauce and beef broth for a juicy and tender finish. This recipe is a flavor explosion in your mouth, and whether you're cooking for a party or just trying to get dinner on the table for the family, these sandwiches are the way to go!

### Serves: 6–8

**FOR THE PORK**

2lb (907g) pork shoulder, trimmed and cut into 3-inch (7.5cm) chunks

1 tablespoon light brown sugar

1 teaspoon chili powder

1½ teaspoons kosher salt

1 teaspoon smoked paprika

1 teaspoon garlic powder

1 teaspoon onion powder

½ teaspoon ground oregano

½ teaspoon ground cinnamon

2 tablespoons avocado oil

1½ cups beef broth

1 tablespoon liquid smoke

1 tablespoon apple cider vinegar

1 cup barbecue sauce

8 brioche buns

**FOR THE SLAW**

½ head of green cabbage, thinly shredded

1 Granny Smith apple, thinly sliced

½ cup shredded carrots

¼ cup mayonnaise

1 tablespoon white vinegar

1 teaspoon granulated sugar

Kosher salt and freshly ground black pepper, to taste

1. In a large bowl, combine the pork, brown sugar, chili powder, salt, smoked paprika, garlic powder, onion powder, oregano, and cinnamon. Massage the seasonings into the meat.

2. In a large saucepan (or in your Instant Pot using the sauté function) heat the avocado oil over medium-high heat. Working in small batches, add the pork to the pan and sear on all sides.

3. Add the pork, beef broth, liquid smoke, apple cider vinegar, and barbecue sauce to the Instant Pot. Close the lid and set the valve to the sealing position before cooking on high pressure for 1 hour.

4. Once done, allow the pressure to release naturally for 10 minutes, then do a quick release to release any remaining pressure.

5. Open the lid and remove the cooked pork shoulder. Transfer it to a large bowl and use two forks to shred the meat.

6. To make the apple slaw, in a large bowl, combine the cabbage, apple, carrots, mayonnaise, and white vinegar. Mix well until combined. Add the sugar, then add salt and pepper to taste.

7. Serve the pulled pork topped with the apple slaw on brioche buns and enjoy!

# SHRIMP FRIED RICE

**PREP TIME: 15 MINUTES • COOK TIME: 20 MINUTES**

Are you in the mood for something that's easy to make yet packed with flavor? Look no farther than this delicious shrimp fried rice! Succulent shrimp, fluffy rice, onions, carrots, and ginger come together in a flavorful Asian-inspired medley that will have you coming back for more. Top it all off with sliced green onions to add a pop of color and even more flavor. For a truly mouthwatering experience, serve with my homemade Yum Yum Sauce (page 195). So why wait? Grab a fork and dig in!

## Serves: 4

1lb (454g) medium shrimp, peeled and deveined

2 teaspoons kosher salt

1 teaspoon smoked paprika

1 teaspoon garlic powder

½ teaspoon ground ginger

1 tablespoon canola oil

3 large eggs, beaten

½ white or yellow onion, diced

1 carrot, peeled and diced

1 tablespoon minced fresh ginger

2 cups of cold, cooked jasmine rice, day old preferably

1 teaspoon sesame oil

3 tablespoons soy sauce

Sliced green onions, green parts only, to garnish

1. In a large bowl, combine the shrimp, salt, smoked paprika, garlic powder, and ground ginger. Mix well and set aside.

2. To a wok or large skillet over medium heat, add the canola oil. Once the oil is hot, add the eggs and softly scramble them. Remove the eggs from the wok and set aside.

3. Add the shrimp to the wok and cook for 3 minutes, flipping halfway through. Remove the shrimp from the wok and set aside.

4. Add the onion, carrot, and minced ginger to the wok. Sauté for 3 minutes or until fragrant and soft.

5. Add the rice and break it down with a wooden spoon while cooking for 2–3 minutes.

6. Add the sesame oil and soy sauce, and mix until every rice grain takes on a light brown color.

7. Toss in the shrimp and eggs and do one final mix.

8. Transfer everything to a serving platter and garnish with green onions before serving.

# TUSCAN SALMON PASTA

**PREP TIME: 15 MINUTES • COOK TIME: 30 MINUTES**

Tender mafaldine pasta coated in a creamy Parmesan sauce and topped with lemon pepper salmon—this combination might not be the most common, but let me tell you, it's the perfect match you didn't see coming. The creamy sauce is made with heavy cream, Parmesan, spinach, and sun-dried tomatoes. The pasta is tossed in the sauce, coating every inch in the cheesy goodness. This recipe is perfect for a satisfying dinner or just in case you need to impress some guests.

## Serves: 6–8

16oz (454g) mafaldine pasta

4 salmon fillets, about 1lb (454g) total, skin on or removed

1 teaspoon lemon pepper seasoning

1 teaspoon kosher salt, plus more

2 teaspoons garlic powder, divided

1 teaspoon onion powder, divided

1 teaspoon smoked paprika, divided

4 tablespoons avocado oil

4 tablespoons unsalted butter

1 shallot, finely diced

½ red bell pepper, diced

5 garlic cloves, minced

2 tablespoons tomato paste

1½ cups heavy cream

1 cup grated Parmesan

4 cups spinach leaves, chiffonaded

1 cup chopped sun-dried tomatoes

Freshly ground black pepper, to taste

3 tablespoons pasta water

1. Cook the mafaldine according to the package instructions. Drain and reserve 3 tablespoons of pasta water. Set the pasta aside.

2. Place the salmon on a baking sheet. Season with the lemon pepper, salt, 1 teaspoon of garlic powder, ½ teaspoon of onion powder, and ½ teaspoon of smoked paprika.

3. To a large skillet over medium-high heat, add the avocado oil. Once the oil is hot, add the salmon and cook for 5 minutes on each side or until fully cooked. Remove the salmon from the skillet and set aside.

4. To the same skillet, add the butter. Once the butter is melted, add the shallot, bell pepper, and garlic. Sauté for 1–2 minutes or until fragrant.

5. Add the tomato paste and cook for 1 minute while stirring. Gradually add the heavy cream while whisking to combine and bring to a simmer. Stir in the Parmesan.

6. Add the spinach, sun-dried tomatoes, the remaining 1 teaspoon of garlic powder, the remaining ½ teaspoon of onion powder, the remaining ½ teaspoon of smoked paprika, and salt and pepper to taste. Stir until the spinach shrinks in size and is fully wilted.

7. Add the cooked pasta to the sauce along with the reserved pasta water and stir until the pasta is fully coated.

8. Serve in bowls topped with cooked salmon and enjoy!

# DINNER FOR TWO

# PENNE ALLA VODKA

**PREP TIME: 15 MINUTES • COOK TIME: 30 MINUTES**

Indulge in a classic Italian American favorite with your special someone with this delicious recipe! Perfectly cooked penne pasta is coated in a mouthwatering tomato-based cream sauce infused with a touch of vodka, creating a surprisingly harmonious flavor combination. The blend of aromatic spices—including garlic, onion, and oregano—complemented by a kick of red pepper flakes creates a taste sensation that will tantalize your taste buds. So, get ready to enjoy a date night favorite and fall in love all over again with this delectable recipe!

## Serves: 2

2 tablespoons unsalted butter

1 tablespoon olive oil

½ white or yellow onion, finely diced

3 garlic cloves, minced

1 teaspoon crushed red pepper flakes

½ cup vodka

1 (14oz [425g]) can of crushed tomatoes

2 fresh basil leaves, chopped

1 teaspoon garlic powder

1 teaspoon onion powder

½ teaspoon ground oregano

½ cup heavy cream

¼ cup grated Parmesan, plus more

Kosher salt and freshly ground black pepper, to taste

½ lb (227g) cooked penne

1. To a large skillet over medium heat, add the butter and olive oil. Once the butter is melted and the oil is hot, add the onion and sauté for 5 minutes or until fragrant. Add the garlic and red pepper flakes and sauté for 1–2 minutes more.

2. Reduce the heat to low and carefully add the vodka. Cook for 3 minutes or until the vodka reduces.

3. Stir in the crushed tomatoes. Add the basil leaves, garlic powder, onion powder, and oregano. Simmer for 10 minutes, stirring occasionally.

4. Add the whipping cream and Parmesan. Stir until the cheese fully melts. Season with salt and pepper to taste.

5. Add the cooked penne and stir until the pasta is fully coated with sauce.

6. Transfer everything to a serving bowl, garnish with more Parmesan, and serve hot.

# PARMESAN-CRUSTED CHICKEN

**PREP TIME: 15 MINUTES • COOK TIME: 15 MINUTES**

Give your taste buds a delicious surprise with this amazing Parmesan-crusted chicken recipe. Each chicken breast is seasoned to perfection, then coated in crispy breadcrumbs and Parmesan before being fried. The chicken is then topped with provolone and baked until melted and gooey. This meal packs a tremendous amount of flavor that's sure to satisfy your cravings. Impress your loved one with this easy-to-follow recipe and enjoy the fine dining taste of a restaurant-quality dish at home.

## Serves: 2

2 (8oz [227g]) boneless, skinless chicken breasts

1 cup all-purpose flour

2 teaspoons kosher salt

1 teaspoon freshly ground black pepper

2 teaspoons garlic powder

2 teaspoons onion powder

1 teaspoon smoked paprika

2 large eggs

¼ cup whole milk

1 cup panko breadcrumbs

1 cup grated Parmesan

½ cup canola oil

½ cup shredded provolone cheese

Fresh parsley, to garnish (optional)

1. Preheat the oven to 350°F (180°C).

2. In a large bowl combine the chicken, flour, salt, pepper, garlic powder, onion powder, and smoked paprika. Massage the seasonings into the meat.

3. In a medium shallow dish, whisk together the eggs and milk.

4. In a separate shallow dish, combine the breadcrumbs and Parmesan.

5. Dip each chicken breast first into the egg mixture, then coat evenly in the breadcrumb mixture.

6. To a large skillet over medium-high heat, add the canola oil. Once the oil is hot, add the chicken and shallow-fry for 4 minutes per side or until golden brown.

7. Transfer the chicken breasts to a baking sheet and top each one with an equal amount of provolone.

8. Place the sheet in the oven and bake for 10 minutes or until the chicken is fully cooked and the cheese is melted.

9. Remove the sheet from the oven, garnish with parsley (if using), and serve hot.

# CITRUS & HERB CREAM CHEESE– STUFFED SALMON

**PREP TIME: 15 MINUTES • COOK TIME: 35 MINUTES**

This stuffed salmon recipe is a personal favorite of mine. Shallots, garlic, spinach, lemon zest, sun-dried tomatoes, Parmesan, and cream cheese are stuffed inside salmon fillets, which are then seared to perfection. Finish cooking the stuffed salmon in the oven until the fillets reach your desired level of doneness. Serve these delicious salmon fillets over a creamy bed of mashed potatoes or fragrant jasmine rice for an amazing gourmet experience.

## Serves: 2

1 tablespoon unsalted butter

1 shallot, diced

2 garlic cloves, minced

1 cup chopped fresh spinach

Zest of ½ lemon

¼ cup chopped sun-dried tomatoes

¼ cup grated Parmesan

8oz (227g) cream cheese, softened

Kosher salt and freshly ground black pepper, to taste

2 (6oz [160g]) salmon fillets, skin on

½ tablespoon Cajun seasoning

1 tablespoon avocado oil

1. Preheat the oven to 350°F (180°C).

2. To a small skillet over medium heat, add the butter. Once the butter is melted, add the shallot and garlic. Sauté until fragrant.

3. Add the spinach and cook until fully wilted and moist.

4. In a medium bowl, combine the cooked spinach, lemon zest, sun-dried tomatoes, Parmesan, cream cheese, and salt and pepper to taste.

5. Use a sharp knife to cut a pocket in the side of each salmon fillet, being careful not to cut through. Fill each pocket with the cream cheese mixture and lightly season with the Cajun seasoning.

6. To a cast-iron skillet over medium heat, add the avocado oil. Once the oil is hot, add the salmon fillets skin side down, laying them away from you. Cook until the skin is crispy, then turn the salmon, cooking the flesh side until nicely seared.

7. Place the skillet in the oven for 15 minutes or until the salmon reaches your desired doneness.

8. Serve with mashed potatoes or jasmine rice and enjoy!

# NEW YORK STRIPS
## WITH MUSHROOM CREAM SAUCE

**PREP TIME: 10 MINUTES • COOK TIME: 20 MINUTES**

This New York strip steak recipe is a mouthwatering masterpiece. You'll begin by searing the steak to perfection in a hot cast-iron skillet, basting it with a mixture of butter, rosemary, thyme, and garlic for added flavor. To elevate the dish further, a delectable mushroom cream sauce with caramelized white mushrooms, cooking wine, and with cream will do the trick. Get ready to savor every bite of this extraordinary dish!

**Serves: 2**

2 (8oz [227g]) New York strip steaks

Kosher salt and freshly ground black pepper, to taste

2 tablespoons grapeseed oil

4 tablespoons unsalted butter

5 whole garlic cloves

1 sprig of rosemary

4 sprigs of thyme

1 cup sliced white mushrooms

¼ cup white cooking wine

1 cup heavy cream

1 teaspoon garlic powder

1. Rest the steaks at room temperature for at least 30 minutes. Pat the steaks dry with paper towels. When the surface of a protein is properly dried, it allows for a crispier sear. Season the steaks with salt and black pepper to taste.

2. Heat a cast-iron skillet over medium-high heat. Add the grapeseed oil, fully coating the skillet. Once the oil is hot, add the steaks, laying them away from you, and press down to make proper contact with the skillet. Cook for 3 minutes on each side or until nicely seared.

3. Add the butter, garlic, rosemary, and thyme. Use a spoon to generously baste the steaks on each sides for 1 minute. (Use a meat thermometer if you need the steaks to reach a desired temperature. Currently, this is aimed for a medium-rare finish.) Transfer the steaks to a cutting board.

4. To the same skillet over medium heat, add the mushrooms and cook until golden brown.

5. Add the white wine and allow it to reduce by ¼ before adding the whipping cream. Bring to a simmer and cook for 3–5 minutes or until thickened.

6. Season the mushroom sauce with the garlic powder, as well as salt and black pepper to taste.

7. Serve the rested steaks with the delicious mushroom cream sauce and enjoy!

# RED WINE–BRAISED SHORT RIBS

**PREP TIME: 30 MINUTES • COOK TIME: 3 HOURS 30 MINUTES**

Indulge in a romantic evening with your loved one and treat your taste buds to the exquisite flavors of these succulent short ribs. Slowly braised to perfection in a rich blend of red wine and beef broth and infused with fresh garlic, onions, and aromatic herbs, such as rosemary and thyme, these short ribs are sure to make your heart flutter with every bite. The tender meat falls off the bone and melts in your mouth, creating an unforgettable dining experience. Make your night special with this delicious recipe and savor the moment with your significant other.

## Serves: 2

3 lb (1.4kg) bone-in beef
  short ribs

1 tablespoon kosher salt

2 teaspoons freshly ground
  black pepper

1 teaspoon garlic powder

1 teaspoon onion powder

2 tablespoons avocado oil

1 white or yellow onion,
  finely chopped

2 large carrots, peeled and
  thinly sliced

2 celery stalks, thinly sliced

5 garlic cloves, minced

1 tablespoon tomato paste

1 tablespoon roasted beef base

2 cups cabernet sauvignon

2 cups beef broth

3 sprigs of rosemary

5 sprigs of thyme

2 bay leaves

1. Preheat the oven to 350°F (180°C).

2. Pat the short ribs dry with paper towels. In a large bowl, combine the ribs, salt, pepper, garlic powder, and onion powder. Massage the seasonings into the rib meat.

3. To a large Dutch oven over medium-high heat, add the avocado oil. Once the oil is hot, add the short ribs and sear on all sides until browned, about 3–4 minutes per side. Remove the short ribs from the Dutch oven and set aside. Don't discard the oil.

4. In the same Dutch oven, add the onion, carrots, and celery. Sauté for 5 minutes or until soft. Add the garlic and sauté for 1 minute more.

5. Add the tomato paste and roasted beef base and cook for 1–2 minutes, stirring continuously.

6. Deglaze the Dutch oven by adding the red wine and scraping up the bottom as you stir for 2 minutes.

7. Add the beef broth, rosemary, thyme, and bay leaves. Add the short ribs, bring to a simmer, then cover the Dutch oven.

8. Place the Dutch oven in the oven and cook for 3 hours. Remove the Dutch oven from the oven and skim the excess fat from the surface of the broth.

9. Serve hot with mashed potatoes or rice.

# HONEY BALSAMIC LAMB CHOPS

**PREP TIME: 10 MINUTES • COOK TIME: 15 MINUTES**

These lamb chops are the perfect combination of savory and sweet. The rich glaze is made with balsamic glaze, honey, and thyme, creating a dish that's simple and tasty. The lamb chops are first seared to lock in the flavor and then coated with the delicious sauce before being baked to caramelize, resulting in an elegant and delicious dish. This is my favorite date night recipe—and it's sure to impress your significant other and have them eating from the palm of your hand.

## Serves: 2

2-4 lamb chops, about 1lb (454g) total

1 teaspoon garlic powder

1 teaspoon kosher salt

½ teaspoon freshly ground black pepper

2 tablespoons avocado oil

¼ cup balsamic glaze

2 tablespoons honey

4 garlic cloves, minced

1 teaspoon dried thyme

1. Preheat the oven to 350°F (180°C).

2. Pat the lamb chops dry with paper towels. In a large bowl, combine the chops, garlic powder, salt, and pepper. Massage the seasonings into the chops.

3. To a skillet over medium-high heat, add the avocado oil. Once the oil is hot, add the lamb chops and sear them for 3 minutes on each side. Remove the chops from the skillet and set aside.

4. In a medium saucepan over low heat, combine the balsamic glaze, honey, garlic, and thyme. Cook for 3 minutes, stirring occasionally, or until the sauce thickens.

5. Generously brush the chops with the sauce. Place the chops on a baking sheet

6. Place the sheet in the oven and bake for 8–10 minutes to allow the sauce to caramelize.

7. Serve hot with the side of your choice.

# NOT THE SAME OLD SIDES

# STIR-FRIED BOK CHOY

**PREP TIME: 10 MINUTES • COOK TIME: 5 MINUTES**

Looking for a tasty way to add some greens to your diet? This bok choy stir-fry will do the trick—and it takes just 15 minutes to make! The bok choy is quickly stir-fried with onions, ginger, and garlic, then coated with soy sauce and sesame oil to add a new depth of flavor. This side dish is loaded with nutrients that are perfect for serving to your family. Be sure to give it a try and let me know your thoughts!

## Serves: 4

1 tablespoon canola oil

½ white onion, sliced

½ red bell pepper, sliced

4 garlic cloves, minced

1 tablespoon minced ginger

1 lb (454g) bok choy, rinsed and ends trimmed

1 tablespoon soy sauce

1 teaspoon sesame oil

1 teaspoon garlic powder

½ teaspoon sesame seeds

Kosher salt and freshly ground black pepper, to taste

1. To a large skillet over medium heat, add the canola oil. Once the oil is hot, add the onion and bell pepper. Sauté for 3 minutes or until soft. Add the garlic and ginger, and sauté for 30 seconds or until fragrant.

2. Add the bok choy and stir-fry for 3 minutes or until the leaves are wilted and the ends are tender.

3. Add the soy sauce, sesame oil, garlic powder, and sesame seeds. Stir to fully coat the bok choy. Season with salt and black pepper to taste.

4. Serve hot as a side and enjoy!

# HONEY BALSAMIC BRUSSELS SPROUTS
## WITH WALNUTS

**PREP TIME: 10 MINUTES • COOK TIME: 35 MINUTES**

This is the perfect side dish to complement any meal. The Brussels sprouts are roasted in avocado oil with salt and pepper, creating a crispy texture. They're then coated with a homemade glaze made from balsamic glaze, honey, and butter, adding the perfect amount of sweetness to the dish. Topped with chopped walnuts and Parmesan cheese, this recipe takes the flavors to the next level. Just make sure to serve hot and enjoy the irresistible combination of sweet and savory—and get the boring out of plain old vegetables!

### Serves: 4–6

1lb (454g) Brussels sprouts, trimmed and halved

2 tablespoons avocado oil

Kosher salt and black pepper to taste

3 tablespoons balsamic glaze

2 tablespoons honey

1 tablespoon unsalted butter

¼ cup chopped walnuts (optional)

1 tablespoon grated Parmesan

1. Preheat the oven to 400°F (200°C).

2. In a large bowl, combine the Brussels sprouts, avocado oil, and salt and pepper, to taste. Toss well. Place the Brussels sprouts on a baking sheet.

3. Place the sheet in the oven and roast the Brussels sprouts for 25 minutes or until tender and browned.

4. In a medium saucepan over medium heat, combine the balsamic glaze, honey, and butter. Stir the ingredients together until fully combined and melted.

5. Remove the sheet from the oven and drizzle the glaze over the top of the Brussels sprouts, coating them generously. Add the walnuts (if using) and Parmesan.

6. Return the sheet to the oven and roast for 10 minutes more or until the glaze is thick and caramelized.

7. Serve hot and enjoy!

# SPICY KALE

**PREP TIME: 10 MINUTES • COOK TIME: 10 MINUTES**

This recipe is the perfect way to add some flavor to your same old greens. A red chili pepper gives a spicy complement to the sweetness from the honey and delivers a great balance of flavor. It's an amazing side that can also work extremely well with your weekly meal prep!

## Serves: 4

2 tablespoons of canola oil

1 red onion, diced

3 garlic cloves, minced

1 bunch of kale, washed and chopped

2 tablespoons of soy sauce

1 tablespoon of sesame oil

1 tablespoon of honey

1 red chili pepper, thinly sliced

Kosher salt and freshly ground pepper, to taste

1. In a large skillet over medium heat, add the canola oil. Once the oil is hot, add the red onion and garlic, and sauté for 3 minutes or until fragrant.

2. Add the kale and cook for 5 minutes or until wilted.

3. Add the soy sauce, sesame oil, and honey. Stir to fully coat the kale.

4. Add the red chili pepper and cook for an additional 2 minutes. Season with salt and pepper to taste.

5. Serve hot and enjoy!

# CHEESY BROCCOLI

**PREP TIME: 10 MINUTES • COOK TIME: 30 MINUTES**

This dish is a delicious and satisfying side the entire family can enjoy. The broccoli is blanched to retain its bright green color and then coated in a creamy cheese sauce made with cheddar and fontina and seasoned with smoked paprika and garlic powder. Baked to a gooey perfection, it's sure to be a flavor explosion. Serve it alongside your favorite protein and enjoy a meal that's guaranteed to impress.

## Serves: 4–6

2 large heads of broccoli, chopped into small florets

2 tablespoons unsalted butter

2 tablespoons all-purpose flour

1 cup whole milk

½ cup shredded cheddar cheese, plus more

½ cup shredded fontina cheese, plus more

1 teaspoon smoked paprika

1 teaspoon garlic powder

Kosher salt and freshly ground black pepper, to taste

1. Preheat the oven to 375°F (190°C). Spray a 9 × 13-inch (23 × 33cm) baking dish with cooking spray and set aside.

2. To a large pot of boiling water, add the broccoli florets and cook them for 3 minutes or until they turn bright green. Drain and transfer the florets immediately to a bowl of ice-cold water to stop the cooking process. Drain the florets again and set aside.

3. To a large saucepan over medium heat, add the butter. Once the butter is melted, add the flour, and whisk continuously for 2 minutes or until the mixture turns light brown.

4. Gradually add the milk, whisking continuously to break up any lumps, and cook the mixture for 5 minutes or until it thickens.

5. Add the cheddar and fontina and stir until the cheeses are melted and the sauce is smooth.

6. Season the mixture with the smoked paprika, garlic powder, and salt and pepper to taste.

7. Add the blanched broccoli to the prepared baking sheet. Pour the cheese sauce over the broccoli and top with more shredded cheese.

8. Place the dish in the oven and bake for 20–25 minutes or until the cheeses are melted and bubbly and the broccoli is tender.

9. Remove the dish from the oven and allow it to cool for a few minutes before serving.

# BACON-WRAPPED ASPARAGUS

**PREP TIME: 10 MINUTES • COOK TIME: 25 MINUTES**

Bacon makes everything taste better, right? This bacon-wrapped asparagus recipe is truly a crowd-pleaser. With a touch of garlic powder, salt, and pepper combined with crispy applewood bacon, this is sure to leave you wanting more.

## Serves: 5

1lb (454g) asparagus, trimmed and washed

2 tablespoons olive oil

1 teaspoon garlic powder

Kosher salt and freshly ground black pepper, to taste

10 slices of applewood bacon

1. Preheat the oven to 400°F (200°C). Line a baking tray with parchment paper or foil and set aside.

2. In a large bowl, combine the asparagus, olive oil, garlic powder, salt and pepper, to taste. Toss well.

3. Bundle 5 asparagus spears together. Use 1 slice of bacon to wrap around each bundle of asparagus and stick a toothpick in the bacon to keep it in place. Place the bundles on the prepared baking tray

4. Place the tray in the oven and bake for 25 minutes or until the bacon is cooked and the asparagus is tender.

5. Remove the toothpicks before serving and enjoy!

# CREAMED SPINACH

**PREP TIME: 15 MINUTES • COOK TIME: 20 MINUTES**

Creamed spinach is one of my favorite side dishes. It's super easy to make, and you can never go wrong with adding it to the family dinner menu. The spinach is blanched and then coated in a delicious scratch cream sauce made from Parmesan and Gruyère, which gives it a rich and nutty flavor. Serve this recipe with dinner or even on its own for a tasty and satisfying meal.

## Serves: 4–6

2 lbs (907g) fresh spinach, washed

2 tablespoons unsalted butter

4 garlic cloves, minced

½ white onion, diced

2 tablespoons all-purpose flour

1 cup heavy cream

½ cup grated Parmesan

½ cup Gruyère cheese, shredded

Kosher salt and freshly ground black pepper, to taste

1. Fill a large pot halfway with water and bring to a boil. Add the spinach and cook for 2 minutes, until wilted. Drain the spinach and blanch it by placing it in a bowl of ice-cold water to stop the cooking process.

2. After 2 minutes, drain the spinach and press out any excess water.

3. To a large saucepan over medium heat, add the butter. Once the butter is melted, add the garlic and onion. Sauté for 2 minutes or until fragrant.

4. Add the flour and whisk until smooth. Cook for 1–2 minutes.

5. Slowly add the whipping cream while whisking to break up any lumps in the sauce. Cook for 5 minutes or until the sauce thickens.

6. Add the blanched spinach, Parmesan, Gruyère, and salt and pepper to taste. Stir to fully coat the spinach in the cream sauce.

7. Serve hot and enjoy!

# LOBSTER MAC & CHEESE

**PREP TIME: 20 MINUTES • COOK TIME: 35 MINUTES**

This dish is loaded with tender chunks of lobster and a creamy blend of cheeses—a combination that's sure to make dinner memorable. With a touch of Cajun spices and Old Bay seasoning, each bite is sure to be just as flavorsome as the next. This is *the* dish you want to share with your loved ones (or treat yourself to).

## Serves: 4–6

2 cups cavatappi pasta

1 tablespoon sea salt

12 tablespoons unsalted butter, divided

4 large lobster tails, chopped into bite-sized pieces (see tip)

4 teaspoons Cajun seasoning, divided

1 teaspoon Old Bay seasoning

3 tablespoons all-purpose flour

3 cups heavy cream

¼ cup shredded chipotle Gouda cheese

1¼ cups shredded cheddar cheese, divided

1 cup shredded mozzarella, divided

¼ cup shredded fontina cheese

¼ cup shredded Gruyère cheese

2 teaspoons garlic powder

2 teaspoons onion powder

2 teaspoons paprika

2 teaspoons freshly ground black pepper

¼ cup panko breadcrumbs

**TIP:** To remove lobster meat from the shell, use kitchen scissors to carefully cut along the soft underside of the tail. Lift the meat gently, keeping it attached at the narrow end, and then place it on top of the shell.

1. Preheat the oven to 350°F (180°C).

2. To a large pot over medium-high heat, add 5 cups of water and bring to a boil. Add the cavatappi pasta and sea salt. Cook for 8–10 minutes, stirring occasionally to avoid sticking.

3. To a large nonstick skillet over medium heat, add 4 tablespoons of butter. Once the butter is melted, add the lobster chunks and cook for 5 minutes. Season with 2 teaspoons of Cajun seasoning and the Old Bay seasoning. Stir well to combine. Remove the lobster from the skillet and set aside.

4. To the same skillet over medium-low heat, add the remaining 8 tablespoons of butter. Once the butter is melted, add the flour and whisk until a paste forms.

5. Gradually add the whipping cream while whisking until combined. Once the cream begins to simmer, remove the skillet from the heat and whisk in ¾ cup of the cheddar, ½ cup of the mozzarella, and all of the fontina and Gruyère. Mix until melted and smooth. Season with the garlic powder, onion powder, paprika, black pepper, and the remaining 2 teaspoons of Cajun seasoning.

6. Add the cooked pasta to the cheese sauce along with the reserved lobster and mix until everything is evenly coated. Transfer everything to a greased 9 × 13-inch (23 × 33cm) baking dish. Top the mac and cheese with the breadcrumbs and the remaining cheddar and mozzarella cheeses.

7. Place the dish in the oven and bake for 25 minutes or until the top is golden brown.

8. Remove the dish from the oven and allow the mac and cheese to cool for a few minutes before serving.

# JALAPEÑO & BACON MAC & CHEESE

**PREP TIME: 15 MINUTES • COOK TIME: 45 MINUTES**

This take on mac and cheese is the ultimate cheesy comfort food with a spicy kick! Loaded with crispy bacon and sautéed onions, jalapeños, and garlic for a delicious aroma, this dish is perfect for a cozy night in or for impressing your coworkers at the next potluck. It's super easy to make and completely delicious. Try this meal out and thank me later!

## Serves: 4–6

8oz (227g) elbow macaroni

6 slices of thick-cut bacon, chopped

½ white or yellow onion, diced

5 garlic cloves, minced

2 jalapeños, seeded and diced

3 tablespoons unsalted butter

3 tablespoons all-purpose flour

1 teaspoon garlic powder

1 teaspoon onion powder

1 teaspoon smoked paprika

Kosher salt and freshly ground black pepper, to taste

2 cups whipping cream

1 cup shredded fontina cheese, plus more

1 cup shredded cheddar cheese, plus more

1. Preheat the oven to 375°F (190°C). Spray a 9 × 13-inch (23 × 33cm) baking dish with cooking spray and set aside.

2. Cook the elbow macaroni according to the package instructions. Drain and set aside.

3. To a large skillet over medium heat, add the bacon and cook until crispy. Remove the bacon with a slotted spoon and transfer to a plate lined with paper towels to soak up any excess grease.

4. In the same skillet, add the onion, garlic, and jalapeños. Sauté for 2 minutes or until soft and fragrant. Remove from the skillet and set aside.

5. In the same skillet over medium-low heat, add the butter. Once the butter is melted, add the flour while whisking until smooth. Cook for 2 minutes.

6. Add the garlic powder, onion powder, smoked paprika, and salt and pepper to taste. Toast the seasonings in the roux for 1 minute before gradually whisking in the cream.

7. Bring the mixture to a simmer and reduce the heat to low before adding the fontina and cheddar while stirring.

8. Add the cooked elbow macaroni, bacon, and sautéed vegetables to the cheese sauce and stir until well combined.

9. Transfer the mac and cheese to the prepared baking dish. Top with more fontina and cheddar.

10. Place the dish in the oven and bake for 20–25 minutes or until the top is your desired amount of golden brown.

11. Remove the dish from the oven and allow the mac and cheese to cool for 15 minutes before serving.

# YELLOW RICE

**PREP TIME: 5 MINUTES • COOK TIME: 35 MINUTES**

Just the smell of this yellow rice is enough to transport you and your taste buds to another world of marvelous flavors. This spice blend paired with basmati rice is tantalizing. This dish is perfect for elevating all your meals with a quick and easy side.

## Serves: 4–6

2 tablespoon avocado oil

2 cups basmati rice

1 teaspoon garlic powder

1 teaspoon onion powder

½ teaspoon kosher salt

1 teaspoon chicken bouillon

1 teaspoon turmeric

1. To a large pot over medium-low heat, add the avocado oil. Once the oil is hot, add the basmati rice and toast for 1 minute.

2. Add the garlic powder, onion powder, salt, chicken bouillon powder, and turmeric. Stir the rice until every grain is evenly coated in the seasonings.

3. Add 3 cups of water to the pot and bring it to a boil. Reduce the heat to low and allow the rice to simmer for 30 minutes.

4. After 30 minutes, turn off the heat and allow the rice to sit for 5 minutes.

5. Fluff the rice with a fork before serving.

# LOADED MASHED POTATOES

**PREP TIME: 10 MINUTES • COOK TIME: 20 MINUTES**

This recipe will become your new favorite side. This classic dish is taken to the next level with the addition of cheddar jack, bacon bits, and green onions. It's the perfect complement to any dinner and so delicious you won't be able to resist going back for seconds.

## Serves: 4–6

2½lb (1.1kg) russet or baby red potatoes, peeled and cut into cubes

Pinches of kosher salt, plus more to taste

1 cup heavy cream

¼ cup sour cream

¼ cup unsalted butter

1 cup grated cheddar jack cheese

1 teaspoon garlic powder

Freshly ground black pepper, to taste

6 slices of bacon, cooked and crumbled, to garnish

2 green onions, chopped, to garnish

1. In a large pot over high heat, add the potatoes with a few pinches of salt and enough water to cover. Bring to a boil and cook for 20 minutes or until the potatoes are fork-tender.

2. Drain the water from the pot and add the whipping cream, sour cream, and butter. Use a masher or mixer to mash the potatoes until smooth and creamy.

3. Add the Cheddar Jack and stir until melted and combined. Add the garlic powder and salt and pepper to taste. Mix until well combined.

4. Serve hot garnished with crumbled bacon bits and green onions.

# STEAK FRIES

**PREP TIME: 10 MINUTES • COOK TIME: 25 MINUTES**

Looking for a simple side dish to pair with your steak dinner? Try these crispy steak fries for a satisfying and easy-to-make option. These oven-baked fries have a perfect soft center and crispy outer layer, seasoned with just salt, pepper, and garlic for a burst of flavor. The best part is, they're also mess-free because you don't need to deep-fry them in oil. Enjoy with one of the dips from this book (see pages 195–205) and be prepared to eat these nonstop.

## Serves: 4

4 large russet potatoes

2 tablespoons avocado oil

1 teaspoon garlic powder

Kosher salt and freshly ground black pepper, to taste

1. Preheat the oven to 425°F (220°C). Line a baking sheet with parchment paper and set aside.

2. Wash the potatoes and cut them into thick wedges.

3. In a large bowl, combine the avocado oil, garlic powder, and salt and pepper to taste. Add the potato wedges and toss until the potatoes are evenly seasoned and coated. Place the wedges on the prepared baking sheet.

4. Place the sheet in the oven and bake for 25 minutes or until crispy.

5. Serve hot with a dipping sauce of choice.

# TWICE-BAKED JUMBO POTATOES

**PREP TIME: 15 MINUTES • COOK TIME: 1 HOUR 15 MINUTES**

Sour cream, butter, cheddar, bacon, potato. Should I continue? These twice-baked jumbo potatoes are the perfect side to your meals. This combination of flavors creates a feast for your taste buds as well as your eyes. Impress your loved ones with this recipe and prepare to have no leftovers.

**Serves: 2–4**

5 strips of thick-cut bacon
2 jumbo baking potatoes
2 tablespoons olive oil
2 teaspoons sea salt
1 cup heavy cream
2 tablespoons sour cream
4 tablespoons unsalted butter
½ cup cheddar cheese,
  plus more
1 teaspoon seasoned salt
2 teaspoons freshly ground
  black pepper
2 teaspoons ranch seasoning
1 teaspoon garlic powder
1 teaspoon onion powder
1 tablespoon chopped
  fresh parsley
Chopped fresh chives

1. Preheat the oven to 400°F.

2. Place the bacon on a baking sheet and place the sheet in the oven for 5–10 minutes. Remove the sheet from the oven and allow the bacon to cool. Once the bacon is cool, place it in a small bowl. Use a wooden spoon to crush the bacon into bacon bits. Set aside.

3. Lower the oven temperature to 350°F (180°C).

4. Clean and brush the baking potatoes under cold water. Dry thoroughly and oil the potatoes with the olive oil. Season the potatoes with the sea salt.

5. Place the potatoes directly on the oven rack with a drip pan on the level below. Bake for 1 hour.

6. Once the potatoes are baked, use oven mitts and cut the top off each potato lengthwise and use a spoon to scoop out the potato flesh .You should have a hollow potato that's almost shell-like when done.

7. Put all the potato filling in a large bowl and add the whipping cream, sour cream, butter, and Cheddar. Stir until well combined.

8. Add the seasoned salt, pepper, ranch seasoning, garlic powder, onion powder, and fresh parsley. Mash until the mixture reaches a mashed potato consistency.

9. Fill the potato shells with the mashed potato mixture, top with more Cheddar, and sprinkle the bacon bits and chives over the top. Place the potatoes on a baking sheet.

10. Place the sheet in the oven and bake for 10 minutes or until the cheese is melted and bubbly.

11. Serve hot.

**DIY**

# YUM YUM SAUCE

**PREP TIME: 5 MINUTES (PLUS REFRIGERATION TIME) • COOK TIME: NONE**

No hibachi night is complete without the perfect yum yum sauce to complement your meal. This creamy and tangy sauce is incredibly versatile and pairs well with everything from sushi to fried rice and noodles. It's also incredibly easy to make: just combine rice vinegar, soy sauce, and a blend of spices to create a delicious depth of flavor that will leave you wanting more. Whip up a batch of this sauce, and try it with my Homemade Shrimp Fried Rice (see page 152). Get ready to take your taste buds on a delicious adventure!

## Makes: 1¼ cups

1 cup mayonnaise

1 tablespoon rice vinegar

1 tablespoon soy sauce

1 teaspoon white granulated sugar

½ teaspoon smoked paprika

½ teaspoon garlic powder

½ teaspoon onion powder

¼ teaspoon ground cayenne

1. In a medium bowl, whisk together all the ingredients. Whisk until fully combined.

2. Taste the sauce and adjust the seasonings to your preference. Pour the yum yum sauce into a Mason jar or any container with an airtight lid and refrigerate for at least 1 hour before using. This will keep in the fridge for up to a week.

# HOMEMADE RANCH

**PREP TIME: 10 MINUTES (PLUS REFRIGERATION TIME) • COOK TIME: NONE**

Nothing beats homemade ranch, and this recipe is versatile and delicious. It's so easy to make with just a few basic ingredients, such as mayonnaise, sour cream, buttermilk, and a blend of spices and herbs, including fresh dill and parsley. This ranch dressing pairs perfectly with every type of dish, especially some hot chicken wings and celery. Try it with one of the delicious appetizers in this book (pages 23–49) and enjoy all the flavors.

## Serving: 1¾ cup ranch

1 cup mayonnaise

¼ cup buttermilk

½ cup sour cream

1 tablespoon minced chives

½ tablespoon minced Italian parsley

1 tablespoon minced fresh dill

1 teaspoon Worcestershire sauce

1 teaspoon garlic powder

½ teaspoon onion powder

¼ teaspoon smoked paprika

Kosher salt and freshly ground black pepper, to taste

1. In a medium bowl, whisk together the mayonnaise, buttermilk, and sour cream. Whisk until smooth.

2. Add the remaining ingredients and mix until well combined.

3. Pour the ranch dressing into a Mason jar and refrigerate for at least an hour before eating. It will keep in the fridge for up to a week.

# REMOULADE SAUCE

**PREP TIME: 15 MINUTES (PLUS REFRIGERATION TIME) • COOK TIME: NONE**

Remoulade is a versatile mayonnaise-based condiment that can add flavor to a variety of dishes. This recipe combines Dijon mustard, garlic, paprika, cayenne, and hot sauce to give the sauce a nice punch of heat. Use it as a topping for fried seafood, vegetables, or my amazing Shrimp Po' Boy (see page 103).

## Makes: 1½ cups

1 cup mayonnaise

2 tablespoons Dijon mustard

2 tablespoons chopped parsley

1 tablespoon minced garlic

1 tablespoon freshly squeezed lemon juice

1 tablespoon Worcestershire sauce

1 teaspoon paprika

¼ teaspoon ground cayenne

1 teaspoon hot sauce (Tabasco recommended)

Kosher salt and freshly ground black pepper, to taste

1. In a medium bowl, whisk together all the ingredients except the salt and pepper. Whisk until smooth and well combined.

2. Taste the remoulade sauce and season with salt and pepper as needed.

3. Cover the bowl with plastic wrap and refrigerate for at least 30 minutes to allow the flavors to meld together before serving.

4. Once the remoulade is chilled, stir the sauce and taste it again. Adjust the seasoning as needed. Store the sauce in an airtight container. It will keep in the fridge for up to a week.

# JERK BBQ SAUCE

**PREP TIME: 15 MINUTES • COOK TIME: 15 MINUTES**

Bring the flavors of the Caribbean to your next backyard barbecue with this homemade jerk sauce. The combination of ketchup, soy sauce, apple cider vinegar, Worcestershire sauce, and honey, along with a touch of my homemade jerk marinade, creates a tangy, spicy sauce that's simmered to perfection. Use it as a dipping sauce for anything from chicken tenders to French fries. The best part is that it's easy to make and can be stored in the fridge for up to 2 weeks, so you can enjoy it for a long time!

## Makes: 1½ cups

1 cup ketchup

¼ cup soy sauce

¼ cup apple cider vinegar

2 tablespoons Worcestershire sauce

2 tablespoons honey

1 tablespoon jerk marinade (see page 53)

Kosher salt and freshly ground black pepper, to taste

1. In a medium saucepan over low heat, combine all the ingredients except the salt and pepper. Mix well and bring to a boil. Reduce the heat to a simmer and cook for 15 minutes, stirring occasionally.

2. Remove the saucepan from the heat and allow the sauce to cool to room temperature. Once the sauce is cool, taste it and add salt and pepper as needed.

3. Store the sauce in an airtight container in the refrigerator for up to 2 weeks.

# KEYSH'S SECRET SAUCE

**PREP TIME: 15 MINUTES (PLUS REFRIGERATION TIME) • COOK TIME: NONE**

Need a tangy twist for your burgers and fries? This easy-to-make secret sauce will do just the trick. Made with a combination of mayonnaise, ketchup, sweet relish, mustard, onions, and a blend of seasonings, this sauce is certified delicious with every bite. Serve as a condiment with burgers, fries, and even chicken tenders.

## Makes: 1½ cups

½ cup mayonnaise

¼ cup ketchup

2 tablespoons sweet relish

1 tablespoon yellow mustard

2 tablespoons finely chopped white or yellow onion

1 tablespoon Worcestershire sauce

1 teaspoon garlic powder

1 teaspoon onion powder

1 teaspoon white granulated sugar

Kosher salt and freshly ground black pepper, to taste

1. In a medium bowl, whisk together all the ingredients except the salt and pepper. Whisk until well combined.

2. Taste the sauce and season with salt and pepper to taste.

3. Cover the bowl with plastic wrap and refrigerate for at least 30 minutes to allow the flavors to combine before serving.

4. Once the sauce is chilled, adjust the seasonings as needed. Store the sauce in an airtight container. This will keep in the fridge for up to a week.

# ISLAND SWEET HEAT BBQ SAUCE

**PREP TIME: 15 MINUTES • COOK TIME: 25 MINUTES**

I accidentally made this sauce one summer two years ago and I've been making it ever since! It's a combination of mango, pineapple, and habanero peppers that slow-cooks in a homemade barbecue sauce for the perfect combination of rich, sweet, and heat. Simply blend all the ingredients together and simmer on the stove for a thick and delicious sauce that has a plethora of uses—from adding some flare to grilled chicken to a juicy rack of ribs. This one will definitely impress your guests at your next cookout!

## Makes: 2 cups

1 mango, peeled and diced

1 cup diced pineapple

1 habanero pepper, seeded and diced

¼ cup apple cider vinegar

¼ cup ketchup

2 tablespoons light brown sugar

2 tablespoons honey

1 tablespoon soy sauce

½ teaspoon smoked paprika

¼ teaspoon ground cumin

Kosher salt and fresh ground black pepper, to taste

1. In a large saucepan over medium heat, combine all the ingredients except the salt and pepper. Mix well and bring to a boil. Once the mixture is boiling, reduce the heat to low and allow to simmer for 25 minutes or until the fruits have softened.

2. Remove the saucepan from the heat and allow the mixture to cool for 10 minutes.

3. Transfer the mixture to a blender and blend on high until smooth.

4. Season the sauce with salt and pepper to taste before using. Store the sauce in an airtight container. This will keep in the fridge for up to 2 weeks.

# HOMEMADE GARLIC & HERB COMPOUND BUTTER

**PREP TIME: 10 MINUTES • COOK TIME: NONE**

Making homemade butter is not only fun but also surprisingly easy. It allows you to enjoy the fresh flavor of butter that can't be replicated in stores. With just a few ingredients and a stand mixer, you can transform a regular bottle of heavy cream into a smooth, herbaceous, and creamy butter you can apply to anything from toast to a juicy steak. This process is super satisfying and extremely fun as a group bonding project, so grab some friends or family and get to it!

## Makes: 2 cups

4 cups heavy cream, at room temperature

6 cups ice-cold water

1 tablespoon sea salt

½ tablespoon finely chopped fresh rosemary

½ tablespoon finely fresh chopped thyme

½ tablespoon minced garlic

¼ tablespoon finely chopped fresh sage

1. To the bowl of a stand mixer fitted with the whisk attachment, add the heavy cream. Start mixing the cream on low speed, gradually increasing the speed to the highest setting.

2. After 3–5 minutes, you'll start to notice the fat from the cream sticking to the whisk and the buttermilk left in the bowl. Transfer the buttermilk to a jar and save it for later use.

3. Remove the butter from the whisk and place it in a large bowl.

4. Pour 2 cups of ice-cold water over the butter and lightly press or knead the butter in the water, pressing out and saving any remaining buttermilk. Pour out the water and repeat this process until the water runs clear (about 3 times total).

5. Drain all water from the bowl and press the butter against the sides of the bowl with your hands or a wooden spatula to remove any excess water.

6. Add the sea salt, rosemary, thyme, garlic, and sage, mixing thoroughly to evenly distribute the herbs. Shape the butter into a cylinder and tightly wrap it in plastic wrap.

7. Chill the butter in the refrigerator until firm, then serve as desired. The butter will last for up to 1 month in the fridge.

# CHIPOTLE-LIME MAYO

**PREP TIME: 10 MINUTES • COOK TIME: NONE**

If you're looking for a way to add some pizzazz to your go-to sandwiches or recipes, this chipotle and lime mayonnaise is the answer. With just a few simple ingredients—including spicy chipotle peppers and tangy lime juice—you can create a perfectly balanced, flavorful mayo that will take your dishes to the next level. Plus, this recipe is incredibly easy to make and can be easily adjusted to suit any crowd size. Use the mayonnaise on a BLT or any sandwich of your choice and enjoy the flavor sensation!

## Makes: 1 cup

1 cup mayonnaise

2 chipotle peppers in adobo sauce, finely minced

1 tablespoon adobo sauce

1 tablespoon freshly squeezed lime juice

1 teaspoon lime zest

2 garlic cloves, minced

Kosher salt and freshly ground pepper, to taste

1. In a medium bowl, whisk together all the ingredients except the salt and pepper. Whisk until well combined. Season with salt and pepper to taste.

2. Transfer the mixture to an airtight container and refrigerate for 10 minutes before use. This will keep in the fridge for a week.

# IN THE MOOD

# FOR SOMETHING SWEET

# PECAN MONKEY BREAD

**PREP TIME: 15 MINUTES • COOK TIME: 30–35 MINUTES**

Get ready to rock your taste buds with this incredibly easy and delicious pecan monkey bread recipe! With just a few simple ingredients and easy steps, you can create a tasty treat that will satisfy everyone's sweet tooth. The cinnamon sugar–coated biscuits are layered in a bundt cake pan and topped with a homemade caramel-pecan sauce, resulting in a warm, gooey, and sticky treat that's irresistible.

## Serves: 10–12

2 (16.3oz [462g]) cans of biscuit dough

1 cup granulated sugar

2 teaspoons ground cinnamon

½ cup unsalted butter

¾ cup light brown sugar

2 tablespoons maple syrup

1 tablespoon pure vanilla extract

1 cup chopped pecans

1. Preheat the oven to 350°F (180°C). Grease a bundt cake pan with nonstick cooking spray.

2. Open the cans of biscuit dough and separate the biscuits into individual pieces. Cut each biscuit into quarters.

3. In a shallow bowl or dish, combine the granulated sugar and ground cinnamon. Mix well.

4. Toss the biscuit quarters in the cinnamon sugar mixture until fully coated. Arrange the coated biscuit quarters in the prepared Bundt cake pan, layering them as you go.

5. To a small saucepan over medium heat, add the butter. Once the butter is melted, add the brown sugar, maple syrup, vanilla extract, and chopped pecans. Stir well until the mixture is smooth and combined.

6. Pour the pecan mixture over the biscuit quarters. Make sure to distribute it as evenly as possible.

7. Place the pan in the oven and bake for about 30–35 minutes or until the bread is golden brown and cooked through (see tip).

8. Remove the pan from the oven and allow the bread to cool for a few minutes.

9. Carefully invert the pan onto a serving plate or platter, allowing the monkey bread to release from the pan.

10. Serve the pecan monkey bread warm, allowing everyone to pull apart the delicious, gooey pieces.

**TIP**: Insert a toothpick into the center of the baked item, and if it comes out clean or with a few dry crumbs, it's fully cooked. Remove it from the oven to avoid overbaking and ensure a moist and delicious result.

# CHOCOLATE CHIP & WALNUT BANANA BREAD

**PREP TIME: 15 MINUTES • COOK TIME: 1 HOUR**

Banana bread is hands down my favorite comfort dessert, and when you add chocolate chips to it, I simply can't resist. This recipe is the ultimate dessert and is guaranteed to warm you right up. You can whip it up in just 15 minutes and then let it bake for 1 hour, filling your home with the delicious aroma of freshly baked bread. This bread is perfectly moist and rich, with a tasty yet subtle crunch from the walnuts. Invite your friends over for a slice—if you can manage to save any!

## Serves: 8–10

2 cups all-purpose flour

½ teaspoon baking soda

1 teaspoon baking powder

½ teaspoon kosher salt

1 cup granulated sugar

½ cup unsalted butter

2 large eggs

2 teaspoons pure vanilla extract

2-3 medium ripe bananas, mashed

½ cup chopped walnuts

1 cup semisweet chocolate chips

1. Preheat the oven to 350°F (180°C). Grease a 9 × 5-inch (23 × 13cm) loaf pan.

2. In a large bowl, whisk together the flour, baking soda, baking powder, and salt.

3. In a separate large bowl, cream the sugar and butter until the mixture is fluffy. Add the eggs one at a time, mixing well after each one.

4. Add the vanilla extract and mashed bananas, then slowly add the dry mixture, stirring until fully combined.

5. Fold the chocolate chips and walnuts into the batter. Pour the batter into the prepared loaf pan.

6. Place the pan in the oven and bake for 1 hour or until a toothpick inserted in the center comes out clean.

7. Remove the pan from the oven and allow the bread to cool for 30 minutes before serving.

# EXTRA-THICK POUND CAKE

**PREP TIME: 15 MINUTES • COOK TIME: 60 MINUTES**

Get lost in this classic dessert recipe for a robust kind of pound cake. With simple ingredients, such as butter, eggs, flour, and sugar, this recipe is not only easy to follow but also yields a rich and moist cake that's perfect for any time of day. The addition of vanilla extract lends a warm and inviting aroma to the cake, and its lightly crisp exterior complements the flavors so well. Finish it off with a dusting of powdered sugar for an elegant touch. Serve with a dollop of whipped cream or fresh berries to add some extra flair to this impressive and delectable dessert.

## Serves: 8–10 depending on size

1 cup unsalted butter, softened, plus more

1½ cups granulated sugar

4 large eggs

4 teaspoons pure vanilla extract

2 cups all-purpose flour

1 teaspoon baking powder

½ teaspoon baking soda

½ teaspoon kosher salt

½ cup whole milk

½ cup powdered sugar

1. Preheat the oven to 350°F (180°C). Grease a 9 × 5-inch (23 × 13cm) loaf pan with nonstick cooking spray or butter.

2. In a large bowl or stand mixer, cream the butter and granulated sugar until fluffy. Add the eggs one at a time, mixing well after each one. Add the vanilla extract and stir.

3. In a medium bowl, whisk together the flour, baking powder, baking soda, and salt. Slowly add the dry ingredients to the wet ingredients. Gradually stir in the milk until everything is combined. Pour the batter into the prepared loaf pan and use a spatula to smooth the top.

4. Place the loaf pan in the oven and bake for 60 minutes or until a toothpick inserted in the center comes out clean.

5. Remove the loaf pan from the oven and allow the pound cake to cool for 20 minutes. Transfer to an elevated wire rack to cool fully before serving.

# LEMON CHEESECAKE

**PREP TIME: 20 MINUTES, PLUS COOLING TIME • COOK TIME: 60 MINUTES**

This recipe takes a classic oven-baked cheesecake and adds a delightful lemony twist to it. With the perfect balance of sweetness and a zesty tang—topped with whipped cream—this dessert becomes the certified main event when you present it at your next family dinner. Get ready to savor each delectable bite because it will disappear before you know it.

**Serves: 8–10, slices depending on size**

2 cups graham cracker crumbs

½ cup unsalted butter, melted

3 (8oz [227g]) packages of cream cheese, softened

1 cup granulated sugar

3 large eggs

½ cup sour cream

¼ cup freshly squeezed lemon juice

Zest of 1 lemon

1 teaspoon pure vanilla extract

1. Preheat the oven to 325°F (165°C). Grease a 9-inch (23cm) springform pan.

2. In a medium bowl, combine the graham cracker crumbs and butter. Stir until the crumbs are moistened. Press the mixture into the bottom of the springform pan to create the crust.

3. In a large bowl, beat together the cream cheese and granulated sugar until smooth and creamy. Add the eggs one at a time, beating well after each addition.

4. Add the sour cream, lemon juice and zest, and vanilla extract. Continue mixing until all the ingredients are well combined and smooth. Pour the batter over the crust in the springform pan, spreading it out evenly.

5. Place the pan in the oven and bake for 60 minutes or until the edges are set and the center is slightly jiggly.

6. Once the cheesecake is baked, turn off the oven and allow the cheesecake to cool in the oven for 1 hour.

7. After 1 hour, remove the cheesecake from the oven and allow it to cool completely on the counter at room temperature.

8. Once cooled, refrigerate the cheesecake for at least 4 hours or overnight for the best results.

# CRÈME BRÛLÉE

**PREP TIME: 15 MINUTES (PLUS REFRIGERATION TIME) • COOK TIME: 40 MINUTES**

Want to add a touch of elegance to your homemade desserts? Indulge in the exquisite delight of crème brûlée. This velvety and rich dessert is a personal favorite, and with just a few simple ingredients, such as egg yolks, sugar, vanilla extract, and, of course, cream, you can create pure magic. But let's not forget about the caramelized sugar topping that forms that irresistible crack when you gently tap it with a spoon. This recipe is perfect for a romancing your date, impressing your guests, or treating yourself to a restaurant-quality dessert in the comfort of your own home. All it takes is a little attention to detail and a touch of patience to create this culinary masterpiece.

## Serves: 4

2 cups heavy cream

1 teaspoon kosher salt

1 tablespoon pure vanilla extract

5 large egg yolks

1 cup granulated sugar, divided

1. Preheat the oven to 325°F (165°C).

2. To a medium pot over medium-low heat, add the cream. Once the cream is simmering, whisk in the salt and vanilla extract until combined.

3. Remove the pot from the heat and allow the mixture to cool for no more than 5 minutes.

4. In a large bowl, whisk together the egg yolks and ½ cup of granulated sugar. Whisk until the mixture forms a velvet icing-like consistency.

5. Gradually add the cream mixture to the egg mixture 1 tablespoon at a time while whisking to prevent scrambling the eggs. Divide the mixture evenly into 4 (4 ounce) ramekins and place them in a baking dish. Pour boiling water into the baking dish until it reaches halfway up the sides of the ramekins.

6. Place the baking dish in the oven and bake for 40 minutes.

7. Remove the baking dish from the oven, remove the ramekins from the baking dish, and refrigerate the ramekins for at least 1 hour.

8. When ready to serve, in a medium nonstick skillet over medium-low heat, create a candy topping by combining 4 tablespoons of water and the remaining ½ cup of granulated sugar. Stir until the sugar dissolves and allow to cook until it turns into an amber-like color.

9. Evenly disperse the melted sugar over the ramekins using a spoon—be careful. Allow the candy to harden before serving.

# CHOCOLATE CHUNK COOKIES

**PREP TIME: 20 MINUTES • COOK TIME: 35 MINUTES**

There's nothing better in this world than a warm chocolate chunk cookie paired with a cold glass of milk! While the process of baking can be intimidating, fear not. This recipe is so easy that anyone can do it. The combination of buttery dough and a copious amount of rich chocolate chunks creates a sweet treat that will satisfy your hunger and cravings. Whether it's a special occasion or simply a part of your daily indulgence, cookies always find a way to bring joy. So don't hesitate to treat yourself to the simple pleasure of baking and indulge in the irresistible allure of homemade chocolate chunk cookies.

### Serving size: 25, depending on size

1 cup unsalted butter, softened

1 cup white granulated sugar

1 cup packed light brown sugar

2 large eggs

1 teaspoon pure vanilla extract

3 cups all-purpose flour

1 teaspoon baking soda

½ teaspoon kosher salt

2 cups chocolate chunks

1. Preheat the oven to 375°F (190°C). Line a baking sheet with parchment paper.

2. In a large bowl, cream together the butter, white granulated sugar, and brown sugar until light and fluffy. Add the eggs one at a time, mixing well after each addition. Stir in the vanilla extract.

3. In a separate large bowl, whisk together the flour, baking soda, and salt. Gradually add the dry ingredients to the wet ingredients, mixing until just combined. Be careful not to overmix.

4. Fold in the chocolate chunks, distributing them evenly throughout the dough.

5. Working in batches, drop rounded tablespoons of dough onto the prepared baking sheet, spacing them about 2 inches (5cm) apart. You can also use a cookie scoop to achieve evenly sized cookies.

6. Place the sheet in the oven and bake for 12 minutes or until the edges are lightly golden.

7. Remove the sheet from the oven and let the cookies cool on the sheet for 5 minutes to firm up the centers. Transfer them to an elevated wire rack to cool completely.

# EASY-TO-MAKE LAVA CAKE

**PREP TIME: 15 MINUTES • COOK TIME: 12–14 MINUTES**

Get ready to indulge in a chocolate lover's dream with this easy-to-make lava cake recipe! These warm and gooey desserts will melt in your mouth and satisfy your craving for something sweet and comforting. They are delicious and simple to prepare, which makes this a fun dish to enjoy with your family. Serve them warm, dusted with powdered sugar, and prepare yourself for a wholesome treat that will leave a lifetime impression on you and your loved ones.

## Makes: 4 cakes

¼ cup all-purpose flour, plus more for flouring

4oz (113g) chopped semisweet chocolate

½ cup unsalted butter

1 cup powdered sugar

2 large eggs

2 large egg yolks

½ teaspoon pure vanilla extract

1. Preheat the oven to 425°F (220°C). Grease and flour 4 (4 ounce) ramekins.

2. In a microwave-safe bowl, combine the chocolate and butter. Melt in the microwave until smooth.

3. In a medium bowl, whisk together the powdered sugar, eggs, egg yolks, and vanilla extract. Slowly pour the melted chocolate mixture into the egg mixture. Stir until smooth.

4. Gradually add the flour to the batter, stirring until just combined. Divide the batter evenly among the prepared ramekins.

5. Place the ramekins in the oven and bake for 12–14 minutes or until the edges are set but the center is slightly jiggly.

6. Remove the ramekins from the oven and allow the cakes to cool for 1–2 minutes. Invert the cakes onto serving plates.

7. Serve warm with a scoop of vanilla ice cream.

# INDEX

## A

## T–U

## V

## W–Z